PROPHETS

in

COMBAT

NICARAGUA

To the countless martyrs of Central America:

Nicaragua, Guatemala, El Salvador, Honduras, Costa Rica,
   Panama.

To their mothers. To their partners, mutilated or abducted.

To all Nicaraguans, my people.

To all those in Nicaragua who are defending their dignity,
   freedom, and peace.
To the *comandantes* and everyone else responsible for public life
   in Nicaragua.
To the leaders of popular organizations,
To those who serve in education and health care.

To the children of Nicaragua and its rebellious youth.

To Christian communities and their leaders.
To the Delegates of the Word.
To the religious and priests who stand by the people in a gospel
   manner.
To the centers for pastoral training and Christian reflection.

To Miguel, Ernesto, and Fernando,
"ministers of God and ministers of the people."

To all those who aid Nicaragua,
with their services, their contributions, their prayer.
To the internationalists,
to independent journalists,
to solidarity committees,
and to sister communities.

And also perhaps to those who have not yet been able to discern
truth, beauty, and gospel
in this Nicaragua of prophets in combat.

PROPHETS
in
COMBAT

The Nicaraguan Journal of
Bishop Pedro Casaldáliga

Translated and Edited by Phillip Berryman

MEYER
STONE
BOOKS

CATHOLIC INSTITUTE FOR
INTERNATIONAL RELATIONS

First published as *Nicaragua: Combate y profecía*,
© 1986 Ayuso - C/San Bernardo, 48, Madrid,
and Misíon Abierta - C/Fernández de los Ríos, 2, Madrid

English translation © 1987 by Meyer•Stone Books

Published in the United States by Meyer•Stone Books,
a division of Meyer, Stone, and Company, Inc.,
714 South Humphrey, Oak Park IL 60304

Published in Great Britain by CIIR
(Catholic Institute for International Relations),
22 Coleman Fields, London N17AF

Cover design: Evans-Smith & Skubic

Cover art: *El pueblo de Boaco*, by Mario Marín

Manufactured in the United States of America
91 90 89 88 87   5 4 3 2 1

Meyer•Stone ISBN 0-940989-02-6

CIIR ISBN 0-946848-94-7

Contents

You must not write a single line
Unless it's about the obsession that won't leave you alone.
— *Ernesto Sábato*

What I have whispered to you,
preach it from the rooftops.
— *Jesus Christ, the Lord*

We've had our chat.
Now
it's time to live like the saints.
— *Leonel Rugama*

Foreword

DRAMA AND POETRY, STRUGGLE AND SONG

São Félix do Araguaia, in the state of Mato Grosso, is one of the most remote and inaccessible places in the vast interior of Brazil. That is where the roads end, and communication becomes impossible. That is also where one of the most impressive pastors in the Brazilian and Latin American church lives, suffers, and bears witness: Pedro Casaldáliga. Out of that solitude come words of fire. Out of those far off places there breaks forth the most direct communication. Distances don't count for mystics, poets, or prophets. They are beyond space and time. They seize the message in the wind and capture the secret meaning of history, especially that history that is overflowing with tears, sweat, and blood. And Pedro is prophet, poet, and mystic.

Prophets in Combat is a field journal covering a period of almost two months. Pedro exercised the "ministry of consolation" and the "ministry of the border" in countless little corners of Nicaragua. In these pages is revealed his soul, volcanic and yet tender. He felt the Spirit's call telling him: the bonds of solidarity with this tiny David being threatened by the giant Goliath must at all costs be strengthened. Nicaragua is being tormented because those who live off the death of others cannot stand the vigor of this tiny seed that bears within it the hope of a whole continent. This little seedling must be watered, fertilized, and enveloped in tender care so it might grow and bear fruit.

Pedro was in Nicaragua representing twenty-three Brazilian bishops and about two hundred church and civic bodies. He did not go there to defy anyone, but to defy fear. He went there to stimulate hope and to confirm his brothers and sisters in the faith.

Cain must not get away with trampling on this plant that is struggling to live and grow. There must be prophetic spirits to bear
witness against iniquity, and prophetic gestures that will cry like
John the Baptist, "You may not do that!"

The whole book exudes combat and prophecy. It relates what
Pedro sees in the everyday life of people who are working, defending their borders from the contra invasion, praying, and mourning
their slaughtered sons and daughters. Pedro is a sharp observer
because he is a mystic. In small gestures, in the expressions he jots
down as they come from the lips of the poor, he discerns all the
wisdom that emerges from suffering. He packs his text with poetry. A remarkable combination it is: drama and poetry, struggle
and song. The "Gospel Insurrection"* is brought into the heart
through conversions, into social structures through the kind of liberation that seeks participation and justice for all — beginning with
the last. And it is brought into the church itself, so that day by
day it may become the people of God by joining the people as they
really are, and as they act in history.

There sits Sandino's hat, ready for anyone who wants to pick
it up and put it on. That means embracing the cause of the liberation of a people that is making history despite its small size,
a people that neither sells out nor surrenders. Pedro took up the
challenge as a Latin American by adoption, as a Christian, and as
a bishop. His being in Nicaragua expressed the real catholicity of
the apostolic mission with which every bishop is invested. Prior
to anything else a bishop is a part of the universal church, which
is the bearer of the cause of Jesus. Every bishop ought to be a
guarantor of this universal mission of Jesus. We do not have many
symbols for making this mission visible and concrete. Pedro's going
to Nicaragua in the name of a large number of colleagues sought
to express the real catholicity of the apostolic mission. It is only
subsequently that the bishop is set into a local church and leads
and guides the journey of a portion of God's people.

In Nicaragua Pedro did not engage in politics. He evangelized.
He fully exercised two ministries that are crucial in that coun-
try: the ministry of consolation and the ministry of the border.
What would become of mothers who bury their children disfigured

---

*National campaign of spiritual renewal that grew out of Nicaraguan foreign
minister Miguel D'Escoto's fast.

beyond human appearance, unless there were someone to console them? What would become of a whole population seeing the noose tightening more and more, sensing the threat of the invasion being prepared, and fearing that the victory of the revolution might be frustrated? Pedro not only provided consolation for those people, but he renewed their hope in the church and in the highest ideals of the Sandinista revolution.

He also exercised the ministry of the border. He stood physically on the border: he put his life at risk. He prayed there and invited everyone to look beyond their borders. He encouraged Christian thought to take on the risk of standing on other borders: how build a society where the starting point is the humble folk? What contribution should Christians make to this huge task? How connect the outer edge or border of politics with the edge of mysticism? What kind of a new church should there be within a new society?

Here Pedro reflects his own broad vision, which has welled up within him during long meditations on horseback, or on the deck of a boat during his long journeys on the Araguaia River, or on foot, as he accompanied lay pastoral agents. Who would have thought that a bishop far from centers of thought and libraries should be able to spell out theory and practice so clearly and insightfully? . . . He fears neither Marxism nor revolution. Those who live imbued with the gospel and with the certainty of the resurrection, those who identify with the poor and even spend their lives committed to full liberation, those who know how to serve the Lord of history in everyday service to the people, receive as gift the serenity and utter freedom of the Spirit. Pedro bears witness that this is not rhetoric but something real and trustworthy.

Today we recall with pride those bishops who during Latin America's colonial period struggled in defense of Indians and slaves, bishops like Julián Garcés, Juan de Zumárraga, Vasco de Quiroga, Bartolomé de las Casas, Antonio Valdivieso, Toribio de Mogrovejo, and others. We are well aware that they were calumniated, persecuted, and exiled, and that some were even murdered. Pedro Casaldáliga continues that line of the forebears of our Latin American faith. Just as it happened to them in their time, Pedro has had to endure misunderstanding and ill will and has had to account for his activities before the church's highest authorities. His response is in the spirit of the gospel: an extra half-hour of prayer each day, fasting on Fridays, and holding a vigil for Nicaragua and Central America every month in his prelature. And — in addition — a solemn promise: should Nicaragua be invaded, he will go back to console and to be on the border, to give his life for his brothers and sisters, as God commands.

Reading *Prophets in Combat* gives us the sensation that we are witnessing a continuation of the Acts of the Apostles. We find battles, but we also feel the joy that springs from the good news. That is why we can make poetry and hold fast to the hope that David will once more defeat Goliath.

LEONARDO BOFF, OFM

Petrópolis, Brazil
June 1986

Preface to
the English Translation

To my friends in the United States
and other friends in the First World:

I'm well aware of how much resistance there may be to a book about Sandinista Nicaragua, especially when it's written by a poor suspect bishop.

In the introductory "Forewarning" I state my position quite plainly. In the book I also state my conviction that "in love, in faith, and in revolution neutrality is impossible."

As a missionary for many years in São Félix do Araguaia in the northern part of the state of Mato Grosso in the Amazon basin of Brazil, I feel deeply Latin American. Nevertheless, I continue to be a man of the First World, even if my beloved old Spain so often seems to be merely a tolerated outpost of that First World....

As a man of the First World I want to ask all my potential First World friends who might read this book to focus on the unquestionable and fundamental principles that we First World people sometimes forget and that the New Nicaragua is elegantly demonstrating before the World Court and before the tribunal of any human conscience that is sensitive to international law, freedom, and peace, the quest of peoples for their own independence and identity, and the equality of all nations.

Freedom cannot remain a statue on a pedestal. It is not the privilege of some supposed mighty ones. The United States is not any "more" than Nicaragua nor is Europe "greater" than Africa.

Augusto César Sandino, general and ancestral forebear, a preeminent figure in the struggle against American imperialism, wrote these prophetic words:

> We ... are not protesting against the magnitude of the inva-
> sion but simply against the invasion. The United States has
> been interfering in Nicaragua's affairs for many years. ... Its
> intervention is more pronounced every day. ... You say the
> governments of Honduras and El Salvador are hostile to me.
> So much the worse for them. Tomorrow they will regret it
> and change their attitude. All Central America is morally
> obligated to unite against the invader. ...

The excuse of anti-communism used by Reagan and others like
him does not in the least justify this aggression, nor the ongoing
imperialism that maintains Central America in subjection, nor the
centuries of colonialism, nor the officially sanctioned poverty, nor
the institutionalized injustice that the ever-servile local oligarchy
maintains over these "lesser" peoples of the empire — once Spanish, then English, now American. You don't defeat communism,
presumably so perverse, with other perversities. You don't prevent
some possible future imperialism — from Russia or wherever — by
using firepower and bloodshed to sustain an imperialist interven-
tion that is evil from any angle. It is more than likely that the
objectives of the Pentagon and the welfare of the White House
will not coincide with the vital necessities and the human rights
of Central America. What's "good" for the United States is not
always good for the rest of the world.

The United States should understand that the cause of Nicaragua is the cause of all Latin America. That Latin America is
ready to say "Enough!" That we don't want to be dominated by
Reagan or the IMF or General Motors or Rambo. We are going
to be brothers and sisters — human persons, sovereign peoples, a
global Humankind — all of us free, all of us equal, each one himself
or herself, all of us together making human history, which is both
arduous and beautiful.

And, speaking in explicitly Christian language, all of us together are bringing about God's Reign.

For this cause of tiny Nicaragua under attack — its people and
its church — is also the cause of God's Reign. This Reign that
is given to us and that we bring about; the Reign of God that
is also the Reign of men and women; the Reign of whites, Indians, and blacks; the Reign of persons and of peoples; a gratuitous
plenitude in the beyond — when the barriers of time and death are

overcome — and a daily conquest in the present, overcoming self-ishness and injustice, overcoming greed for profits and the arrogant might of weapons.

•

This book is written by a Christian who is a bishop. With my limitations and enthusiasms, reader, but also with the co-responsibility that I have accepted for the church. For I believe that Nicaragua's cause is also the cause of the whole church of Jesus. A symbol-case, a crucial locus for experiencing both faith and politics harmoniously and dialectically, its past one of a more or less colonizing and oligarchical Christendom, and its future a Christianity that will be more evangelizing and rooted in the people; a prototypical locus for keeping lit the flame of the credibility of the church that is *semper renovanda* — and ultimately the credibility of Jesus and of his Father our God, above and beyond the contingent aspects of a revolutionary process in history.

Just as there is a First World, there is a First Church — and they have their counterpart Third World and Third Church. The First Church must comprehend and joyfully accept that the Third Church will finally be itself, faithful and indigenous, "catholic" and different, so that, in the unity of faith and the plurality of communion, both may be followers and messengers of the Word of God who became incarnate in a time and a country (indeed, in a country colonized by another Empire!).

I want to tell Christians and specifically Catholics that there is no so-called popular church — schismatic or headless — in Nicaragua, such as Nicaragua's enemies, for their own reasons, or some narrow-minded and nearsighted people, have sought to detect with alarm. Yes, there is a portion of the church of Jesus — both Catholic and Protestant — that strives to be faithful to the historic demands of his people, precisely in the name of the gospel. There is a tension — which will be healthy in the long run if many of us get involved with our hands and on our knees — that will force both sides to pluralistic dialogue, to accepting the complementarity of charisms and services, to the realistic dialectic of history, to fidelity to the signs of the times and of the place. All of which meshes perfectly with the spirit of Vatican II, if I may point to an expression of the church at the highest level.

If these arguments and demands and examples are not enough,

I must remind my friends in the United States and in the whole First World that in Nicaragua, in Central America, and throughout this whole Great Homeland of this continent to the south, there is a vast flood of people, a whole legion of those "marked with blood," a legion "that no one can count" who are making their claim. These people are judging us with the absolute legitimacy of their extreme witness. It is to this witness in blood that my fragile witness on paper makes its appeal. . . .

PEDRO CASALDÁLIGA, CMF

São Félix do Araguaia, Brazil
January 1987

Forewarning

For the title of this book, I had thought of using the moving verse of the song "Ay, Nicaragua, tiny Nicaragua" [*"¡Ay, Nicaragua, Nicaragüita!"*]. My feeling toward Nicaragua arouses an anxious "Ay!" deep within me. Facing the ominous threat hanging over it, as people and as church, suffering ever-growing aggression from mercenary armies, oligarchical interests, and counterinformation; subjected to an economic boycott and many-leveled encirclement; prevented from being itself by the powers that be, in the name of the empire and its gods. My feelings about Nicaragua come out in the diminutive form for tenderness — *"Nicaragüita"* — as something that's very much my own, a love that belongs to us all, a problem and legacy that's within our own house, the cause of the tiny "Tom Thumbs" of the continent — Central America and its slaughtered peoples — the "little ones" of history and God's Reign.

"Prophets in Combat" will be the title of this book since that's what Nicaragua is all about.

•

Writing a book always means not writing another. Making choices, ignoring, editing down. I will leave unsaid many things I would like to say. I will not be able to draw as clear a picture as it might be desirable to do since the topic is so utterly polemical on all sides, as this tiny and huge Nicaragua today: Politics and Church, Religion and Society, Socialism/Sandinismo and Social-Christian-Democrat neocapitalism. . . . The new and the old in dialectical, mysterious confrontation. Truths, lies, and passions all mixed together in ambiguity.

My pace as a bishop doesn't give me much quiet time for writing. One has to write on the go.

This book is a wad of diary notes, not yet dry. A diary in the

1

"mountains," on the "border," in "insurrection." They're notes I took as I went along, usually on scraps of paper that got soaked in the rain more than once. Real notes, that's for sure. I accept responsibility for them.

Of course, I'll say what I saw and heard, as I saw and heard it.

While still in Nicaragua I sent an article on my experiences during those days of "Gospel Insurrection" to a number of papers and magazines in the Americas and Europe. It began like this:

Many others have seen Nicaragua. Each one with his or her own eyes. Some have looked on it as a show; others as a mystery or something ambiguous or scandalous; or as a beautiful challenge.

I came away from Nicaragua with "a garden of aches and tender feelings," as I put it in that introduction.

That is how I've seen it, how I've felt it, how I've taken it on: as a marvelous challenge, a human commitment, a Latin American adventure, co-responsibility in the church. A commitment that commits, but one as inescapable as a gospel passage — as when the living God "passes" through the midst of the Poor of the Land, as a history-making hour of God's Reign.

•

I'm saying out loud — for anyone who still believes in my witness — what I could not in conscience leave unsaid. This book is a duty. Neither as a human being, nor as a Latin American, nor as a Christian and bishop, do I want to sin by omission.

•

I have no intention of canonizing things that are contingent and stormy, as is the case with anything human and temporal. Those who are in charge of such processes and believe their cause is without sin may cast the first stone — and I include the process of the church as well.

I beg potential readers who have already made up their minds against the new Nicaragua and against that Nicaraguan church that stands alongside the people, experiencing their pain and hope, not to read this book. For it is written from the other side: in favor. And because you can't read with your eyes closed.

I ask all who have Latin American eyes and ears and hearts to
see and hear and feel and respond in a Latin American way.

I ask all those who love the cause of Nicaragua and of all Central
America to defend it with whatever means they have at hand. The
situation is urgent.

And, besides acting I ask all those who believe in the God of
Life and Liberation also to pray that God's Reign may continue to
occur in Nicaragua.

Tomorrow may be too late, at least for us: for this day of
Nicaragua is also our day.

●

As a further "forewarning," for myself first of all, yet another poem:

You are costing your own best people ever more
— so much blood and waiting! —
you will no doubt cost me a lot
                    Nicaragua
                            most dear,
                    Sandino and Gospel.

But I don't regret loving you.

I won't ignore the dead I've seen in your mountains,
the snares that surround your borders,
the sobbing I've held in my arms,
the pine flame enkindled in your eyes,
Nicaragua, chosen to be the New Time,
embattled prophecy.

Notes from an Emergency Diary

Gospel Insurrection

Miguel D'Escoto, the foreign minister of Nicaragua and a Maryknoll priest, is on a "hunger strike," say the media; on a gospel fast, to put it more accurately. It's now been seventeen days. For peace and self-determination in Nicaragua and all Central America; a sacrifice made in faith and in solidarity with all these populations undergoing martyrdom; issuing a call to the church and people of the United States; crying out to the world.

Maybe I should go to Nicaragua to join in this vigil of Miguel D'Escoto. With our patriarch Sergio Méndez Arceo,* with Adolfo Pérez Esquivel,† with other friends in solidarity.

Our insensitivity, ideological excuses, and ecclesiastical fastidiousness neutralize love and witness ...

•

On my way through Goiânia, stopping at the national office of the Pastoral Land Commission, I learn about one more martyrdom: Father Ezequiel Ramin, an Italian missionary, here in Brazil a little more than a year, has been ambushed and murdered by a landholder's gunmen. It happened in the diocese of Ji-Paraná, Rondônia.

I'm on my way to Nicaragua.

---

*Retired bishop of Cuernavaca, Mexico.

†Argentinian coordinator of a Latin American nonviolence network; Nobel Peace laureate.

The paper says that from Lima Gustavo Gutiérrez* has joined Miguel's fast.

A Contadora of the Spirit is coming into being. May the Spirit be with us, bright and strong. With the Spirit we can really set in motion this "Gospel Insurrection" Miguel dreams about.

Yolanda, the Mexican who works with CEPA† in Nicaragua, just passed through São Félix. She gave me a brightly colored sash, a marvelous piece of work done by Guatemalan Indians. I'm taking it to Nicaragua as a paschal stole of martyrdom, knitting us in solidarity with all our inflamed Central America.

•

Both ambassadors — Nicaragua's, Ernesto Gutiérrez, a great poet and old friend, and Spain's, Miguel Aldasoro — treat me very cordially and efficiently. In a few hours I take care of my passport, which has lain dormant since that day I arrived in Brazil, seventeen years ago. Being a bishop and more or less passing as a revolutionary still brings some privileges. And also disadvantages. The police — unmistakable with their scarcely disguised insolence — did everything they could to listen in on our conversation in the Goiânia airport. The "New Republic" holds on to old ways.

•

I get my passport pictures in a shop in the bus station in Brasília. In "twenty minutes" — they claim — they give you back your face, looking startled and stupid, forever.

The owner of the shop could be an English Protestant. "When a man is tired of London he is tired of life" (Dr. Samuel Johnson), says the tourist poster — with spires and the Thames. Alongside it, in much more discreet letters on a green and gold plaque the apostle Paul states, "If anyone is in Christ, he is a new creature." Both in London and away from London, I presume . . .

•

The Spanish imperial eagle is gone from the passport, replaced by a solemn royal crown. When their time comes, empires pass away.

The passport is "valid for every country in the world" until "July 25, 1990," which is also the feast day of the country's patron,

---

*Peruvian theologian, author of *A Theology of Liberation* (Orbis, 1973).

†A training institute for Christian peasant leaders.

St. James. It may be that by that time a passport will no longer
be necessary.

●

On July 27 I put out a communiqué with the list of the twenty-
three bishops, two Protestant pastors, and more than two hundred
organizations and individuals who, after a simple invitation, chose
to support my gesture of solidarity with Father D'Escoto's vigil:

> As a Latin American by adoption and as a Christian and
> bishop, in the name of the church of São Félix do Araguaia,
> Mato Grosso, Brazil, and as a delegate of my brother bish-
> ops and their churches, and of the Protestant brethren and
> the organizations and individuals listed below, I am going to
> Nicaragua to join in the prayer and fasting of Father Miguel
> D'Escoto and the tense vigil of his people.
>
> I believe this action of mine is inspired by the gospel. For
> peace, for non-intervention in Nicaragua and Central Amer-
> ica, for the self-determination of these peoples. To jolt the
> conscience of the First World with the drama and the tram-
> pled rights of Central America and of the whole Third World.
> In order to share in co-responsibility for the church of Jesus,
> in making it more credible, in this martyred Central America
> and throughout Latin America.
>
> "Some devils," says the Lord, "can only be cast out by
> means of prayer and fasting."
>
> "Gold and silver I have none," I could say, along with Pe-
> ter and John; neither arms, nor diplomacy, nor power. "What
> I have, that will I give you": the prayer of my Christian faith,
> my Latin American passion, unquenchable hope in the Lib-
> eration of God's Reign, and, if need be, along with so many
> others who have gone before us, my own life as well. "In
> the name of Jesus of Nazareth, Nicaragua, Central America,
> Latin America, arise, as yourselves, free of interventions, and
> walk in the breeze of the New Freedom!"

On the same day, I also wrote to the presidency of the CNBB
(National Commission of Brazilian Bishops):

> I am on my way to Nicaragua. I am going to join the vigil of
> prayer and fasting of Father Miguel D'Escoto and the larger

vigil of his whole people, and of the peoples and churches of all Central America.

Twenty-three brother bishops support me in this mission of solidarity, as do many other organizations and friends.

For peace, for non-intervention, for the self-determination of Nicaragua and of Central America.

I am communicating this personal decision to the presidency of the CNBB in a spirit of fraternal and apostolic co-responsibility.

I also trust you will pray for me.

The Lord Jesus and the Mother of Guadalupe, patroness of our Latin America, will keep watch over her poor, over the journey of our churches, over the coming of God's Reign, which is also, beginning even now, justice, freedom, equality, and peace . . .

•

I am in Nicaragua, in this Nicaragua engaged in vigil.

At the outset, I must repeat those lines of Antonio Machado, extending them collectively to the whole continent:

> Hour of my heart,
> the hour of a hope
> and a despair.

Church of God, what do you have to say for yourself? What do you have to say about God in this Nicaragua under attack and struggling for peace?

What do you have to say about Nicaragua, Western society?

What do I have to say, what am I doing here, bishop that I am?

Nicaragua is a mystery (of grace and of iniquity, and I don't exactly mean Sandinista iniquity . . .). It is also a volcano. The whole place is a Momotombo.* And it is a poem.

I've just arrived, only a week ago, but already it feels like a century to me.

In the airport in the rain, I am met by friends from the Centro Valdivieso, from CEPA, from *El Tayacán*.† Friends I've known from afar, but close because they're deep in my heart.

---

*Large volcano, often referred to in Nicaraguan poetry.

†Centro Valdivieso, pastoral-theological reflection and training center.

Then I embrace Miguel. Along with his hug, Miguel D'Escoto, the prophet institutionally blocked, shows me his eyes, pained with anxiety, like two votive candles flickering among statues. His faster's beard, sprinkled with gray, has now grown out.

In answer to my embrace, Miguel pours out his feelings to me, full of distress, "Pedro, the contras killed eight of our mothers today, while they were on their way into the hills with baskets of food for their children on combat duty."

I have supper and sleep at Uriel Molina's house, taken in with Franciscan hospitality and surrounded by moving symbols. Already on this first Nicaraguan night, I am inundated with references, intuitions, challenges.

•

The following day in León I concelebrate the funeral — dramatic, huge — held for these mothers just killed. President Daniel Ortega also attends the funeral.

"Esteemed American leaders, esteemed congressional representatives who voted the $27 million for the contras, don't be so cynical!" Daniel would shout later in the public ceremony out in the open. "Does murdering mothers, women, young people promote democracy and human rights in Nicaragua? Don't fool yourselves: the people will never betray the memory of these mothers, sisters, and spouses."

"The women yelled at the contras in desperation: 'Cowards, don't kill us, we're mothers!'" recalls Rufina Betanco Ramos, recreating the most heart-rending moments of the ambush by mercenaries.

"Before killing them," says the one survivor, Nubia Vargas, who works in the Alinsa factory, "They grabbed some of them, raped them, and then cut off their legs and chopped them up."

The caskets are there, across from the altar. And I feel that the altar and caskets are a single Pasch. I kiss the altar and kiss the caskets, along with the other concelebrants. I console the victims' families, and I address the people:

"I bless you in the blood of Jesus and in the blood of these mothers whom I declare to be resurrected.... May the God of Life,

CEPA, Center for Rural Education and Training, training center for rural Christian leaders. *El Tayacán*, publication popularizing position of Christians involved in the revolution.

the God of Freedom, and the God of Peace bless you all!"

"... Nicaragua's hope will not be in vain, for the God of the poor will not allow them to destroy it."

The lines of Edwin Castro, engraved on a wall in the streets of León, take on a maternal resonance within me that day:

> Tomorrow, dear mothers,
> everything will be different ...

Those mothers, who once gave birth to children, were now, in simplicity and heroism, giving birth to the new Nicaragua.

In the afternoon, I also concelebrate in the town of La Trinidad, another funeral, this one for thirty soldiers fallen in the flower of youth.

For someone just arrived it has been a powerful baptism of bloodshed and grief!

•

Around Managua — although I can't enjoy it given the dramatic circumstances of my arrival — extends the green beauty of my first contact with this Nicaragua still in the midst of the rainy season. And the lakes. And the sea.

> I suspect there are so many poems
> in your eyes, Nicaragua
> that we'll hold onto them
> for when the mountains
> find themselves at peace ...

The heat is more humid than in my own Mato Grosso. You feel the pressure. There is a lot of pressure bearing down on everyone's life, on the whole atmosphere in this troubled hour of Nicaragua.

•

This is the news people want to know, so I explain it to them: "I've come to join Miguel's fasting and prayer for peace, for non-intervention in Nicaragua and in Central America, and for the self-determination of these peoples."

These words became a constant refrain during those first few days of the Gospel Insurrection.

I have also come, as a Latin American bishop, to contribute my co-responsibility for the sake of the credibility of the church in Nicaragua, in Central America, in Latin America, within these processes of social transformation, of affirming the identity of our countries, of independence.

I have come to be close to the suffering of these people.

... Yes, even to make up a little — without any pretensions but consciously — something that perhaps is lacking here in "the Body of the Lord that is his church."

I know that my coming is a "sign of contradiction." That is not my intention, but I can't avoid it. In any case, the cause of Jesus, whether we serve it better or worse, always puts us "in violence," as he foresaw. And at any moment God can call out to us from a burning bush.

This is certainly a break from my usual life in Brazil. It's something that just overwhelmed me. I've been in Brazil for more than seventeen years and never left, not even when my mother died back in Spain.

The "Gospel Insurrection" that Miguel has set in motion is a kind of "Contadora of the Spirit." All the other battle trenches, which he admits are certainly necessary — regrettably necessary, he says of them — have not been enough. This other trench, theological, evangelical, had to be set up.

It is a prophetic sign. Gratuitous. Miguel is insistent on this aspect of gratuitousness. Gospel gratuitousness, however, does not do away with that political effectiveness toward which an integral liberation ought to strive as well. The effectiveness of God's Reign, itself already a gift, still a promise and yet something to be sought for and won.

The gratuitousness of faith can be combined — in a higher dialectic — with the effectiveness of real politics, even when it always goes beyond politics. Jesus asked us to regard ourselves as — but not to be! — "useless servants." "As though everything depended on us, all the while aware that everything depends on God," as the Ignatian formula puts it.

At another press conference, to sum it up, I tell the media people — Nicaraguans and foreigners — that I have come to Nicaragua because of Chapter 25 of St. Matthew's Gospel.

In the church — which is not monolithic, thank God, and is even contradictory in its varying stances, I point out to the journalists, catechizing — there must be room not only for communion within pluralism, but also for effective communion with peoples and their processes in history, especially when it is a case of peoples that are both oppressed and believing.

Sincerity is more important than understanding with Cartesian clarity. And solidarity must not tolerate too many delays. Solidarity, which Giaconda Belli* calls "the affection of peoples," ought to be an ongoing, effective charism of the church.

The last two superiors general of the Jesuits have been advising their missionaries in Nicaragua and elsewhere in Central America to offer a "critical support." Nothing more, but nothing less, either. Perhaps I'm going to give more ...

I know I'm being accused of butting into other people's business. Although some, perhaps many, do not understand me, I don't think I can ignore that question of the Lord, "What have you done with your brother, for your brother?"

You can be a Cain by killing, but you can also be a Cain by allowing others to get away with killing.

I write the Nicaraguan bishops a letter to, as it were, justify what I'm doing. I arrived the night of July 28, 1985; the two emergency funerals on the 29th prevented me from writing them on the first day of my stay in Nicaragua, as I had intended. I write the letter on the 30th.

I have thought it over, prayed, and consulted with others. It strikes me as better to write to them without going to see them first. So as not to lay conditions on them, nor on me either. Although canon law gives bishops certain broad faculties, I realize that canon law might come off badly with my visit to Nicaragua. I pray the Lord that the gospel won't come off badly.

•

To Archbishop Obando y Bravo,
Cardinal of Managua,
and to the whole Nicaraguan Bishops Conference.

Dear Brothers:

On Sunday the 28th I arrived in Managua in order to join the vigil and fasting of Father Miguel D'Escoto and the anxious vigil of the entire people and the churches of Nicaragua.

To me it seemed to be a call from God in my life as a

---

*Poet and longtime Sandinista militant.

bishop; and the pastoral team of my church of São Félix do Araguaia fully supported my decision.

I felt that this gesture could be a small contribution to the solidarity of Latin America, and more specifically of Brazil, with Nicaragua and all of Central America; an appeal to the conscience, human and Christian, of the First World; an ecclesial service of apostolic co-responsibility.

I have not come to teach any lesson. I want to be near the suffering and hope of your people.

My attitude could be conflictive; it is so for me as well: the cause of God's Reign always demands "violence" of us. In any case, my intention is sincerely inspired by the gospel.

I am enclosing the note with which I explained my decision to the church and people of Brazil as well as the letter I sent to inform the presidency of our bishops conference, along with the list of the twenty-three bishops of Brazil who, in just one day of contacting, joined me in solidarity, delegating to me their complete support and the support of their churches. Some two hundred bodies and individuals in Brazil — pastoral teams, human rights groups, labor unions, native peoples organizations — also made me their delegate in solidarity.

I beg you, brothers, to accompany me with your prayer. The Lord Jesus is always there where we unite in his name. Mary, his mother, who suffered like so many Nicaraguan mothers and is today in glory with her risen Son, will not fail to open her heart to this cry for peace from a whole people, which joins this national effort at life and liberation.

I embrace you fraternally, in Christ Jesus ...

That same day, July 30th, Bishop Bosco Vivas Rabelo, as secretary of the Nicaraguan Bishops Conference, signed a letter addressed to the president of our Brazilian Bishops conference (CNBB), Archbishop Ivo Lorscheiter. This letter got to *O Estado de São Paulo*, a conservative paper and longtime foe of the CNBB, before it reached the bishops conference. The message reads:

The bishops of the Nicaraguan Bishops Conference greet their brother bishops of Brazil and ask them to respect the authority of the local bishops by avoiding any interference that may make matters worse for the church in Nicaragua, which has already suffered a great deal. The Nicaraguan bishops know the situation of their church and their country better than the Brazilian bishops, since they experience the anguish and hopes along with their faithful. The bishops of Nicaragua believe that the charity and communion of the church are gravely damaged when some bishops of Brazil speak or act in disregard for the authority of the Nicaraguan episcopacy.

The general secretary of the Brazilian Bishops Conference answered in the name of the CNBB, acknowledging the Nicaraguan bishops' right to register their complaint but also respecting— "profoundly," he said — my gesture of solidarity with the Gospel Insurrection.

•

There are four things I've already come to understand: First: truth is on Nicaragua's side. It is Nicaragua that is under attack: from Reagan's policy in the U.S. — from outside. There is no "civil war" in Nicaragua. To say or think such a thing would reflect a stupidity or a perverse complicity.

Second: This revolutionary process (and here the word "revolution" takes on tones and values that are both matter-of-fact and necessary), even with its faults and unanswered questions, is today the best alternative for Nicaragua — for the Nicaraguan people. For the empire's appetite in Central America and Latin America, it's no doubt the worst alternative, as it is for the status of the servile and privileged groups.

I also believe, seeing things with my own eyes and believing on the basis of what I'm seeing, that this alternative — contingent, fragile perhaps, and mixed with impurities — in its social, economic, political, and even cultural aspects, is potentially more in accordance with the program of the gospel.

Third: the Nicaraguan bishops may — even should — keep their distance, an evangelically critical distance, from the revolutionary political process. Nevertheless, I do not think they can do anything but openly condemn Reagan's imperial aggression. I also believe they should join — even lead in the name of the gospel — this national campaign for peace, which is sealed every day with weeping and blood. I believe they should celebrate the Eucharist for all the people who die as a result of this aggression and do it without reserve: they should weep with the mothers and orphans and show their mercy by being with the wounded, and they should demand that those who have been abducted be returned.

I also think that at this moment, with all its importance for history and for the church, all the bishops of Central America should respond by publicly taking a joint position, explicitly denouncing the aggression, the genocide, the manipulation, the long-standing policies of subjection that weigh tragically over their peoples. They should demand for those peoples that their dignity as nations be respected, that the truth be known internationally, and that full self-determination be achieved.

Fourth: the route to the impending future of Latin America and the Latin American church is to be found today in Central America, and more specifically in Nicaragua. Tomorrow it will be too late. And if we fail to measure up, once again we will have been accomplices, at least by remaining silent, because we were afraid of prophecy, because we were unwilling to dirty our hands in the turbulent waters of history.

•

Mothers besiege me, asking for blessings for their children in the hills. Like Rachel, they recall their dead children. With this overflowing cordiality that is so Nicaraguan, simple people thank me for being here in solidarity, for the consolation I offer them, and for confirming their abused faith by being here as a bishop.

The letter from Cardinal Paulo Evaristo Arns, archbishop of São Paulo, has been a blessing from God over Nicaragua. Everyone is saying it is a history-making event. Dom Paulo addresses his letter "My dear friend Miguel":

> "One does not live by bread alone, but by every word that comes from the mouth of God" (Matthew 4:4).
>
> This message of Jesus, after he had spent forty days fasting in the desert, sheds light on the event in which you are the leading figure. Jesus engaged in this fast to show his commitment, his openness to the will of the Father, before setting out on his liberating apostolic mission.
>
> Your fast under present circumstances is alerting the ethical conscience of the world to the grave situation the people of your country are experiencing. Your prophetic gesture de-

nounces the efforts to kill the seed of new life planted by the Sandinista revolution.

I have a great deal of respect for your decision to carry out this fast, inspired by your "priestly conscience faced with the reality of death and destruction taking place in Nicaragua, as a result of the war of aggression that the government of the United States has declared against us."

Your country has the right to choose the best possible route toward more just living conditions for the people, without interference from a foreign power. The self-determination of your country is essential to the peace and harmony of our Latin American continent.

I am taking advantage of the occasion to remind the United States government that the aspirations of the Nicaraguan people to freedom and peace are legitimate and noble, and to unite myself in solidarity with your people in the struggle to build a new society where people may live as brothers and sisters in justice and peace.

As a brother, I beg you to consider the possibility of ending this gesture if it comes to the point where you feel your life is in danger, since both we and your own people cherish and value that life.

The letter is dated July 23. On August 8, Bishop Mathias Schmidt, an American Benedictine and bishop of Ruy Barbosa, in the arid Northeast of Brazil, sent me another letter, which is also quite meaningful, both for its content and because it is an American who wrote it:

I'm in Goiânia taking part in the CPT (Pastoral Land Commission) Assembly. I'm taking advantage of Ricardo's trip to send along my own embrace and solidarity.

I want to join with you, with D'Escoto, and with the people of Nicaragua in this dramatic moment when life and death hang in the balance. I would like to be physically present to take part in this gesture of gospel solidarity.

As an American citizen I feel ashamed over what the government of my country is doing in order to destroy a people that is struggling for its own liberation. As a Latin American bishop I join the suffering of this despoiled nation and all the Latin American peoples in their struggle against this exploitation. I believe in the Resurrection, the guarantee for our Hope.

I embrace you with a fraternal embrace, one that reaches out to the people of that beloved country.

•

At the Red Cross I visit the mothers who are fasting for their children, rural schoolteachers who were abducted by the contras. The young people — girls and boys — are members of the "50th Anniversary" Teaching Brigade. Their mothers have just sent an S.O.S. throughout Nicaragua and around the world. They personally hand me an agonizing letter: "In the few days you have been in our beloved Nicaragua you have experienced how bitter is the unjust war that imperialism thrusts upon us. You have witnessed the suffering that inflicts so much destruction and death on us. This is unjust, but God is just...."

In the name of these sorely afflicted mothers and at their request, I send letters, with enough documentation enclosed, to the archbishops of Tegucigalpa and San José. There are reports from many reliable witnesses that these young teachers who were carried off by force are being held in Honduras and Costa Rica. "Held by force in contra camps in both those countries," say the mothers, adding in the S.O.S. "the governments of Honduras and Costa Rica are accomplices, since they remain silent in the face of these acts that violate human rights."

In La Trinidad, after that first funeral mass on the afternoon of my first day in Nicaragua, a mother, both strong and sorrowful, embraced me. "One of them is my son, bishop; another son of mine fell two weeks ago. And there's also a nephew of mine who was killed. But I know they have not lost their lives: they were working in the Lord's vineyard."

Like so many other young people or adult men, they were Delegates of the Word, leaders of the Christian community. If it were valid to distinguish between one kind of blood and another — all of it human blood — we could remind the ecclesiastics, who are fastidious and too confined to their own house, that here and throughout Central America much "blood of the church" is being spilled ...

•

Thus says the Lord to them:
If I had not come
they would not be to blame.
But I came in these dead ones
in the Peace for which the people cry out,
in the whole country at war,
in this burning vigil,
in the mass they still celebrate.
If I had not come ...
but I came:
    see my wounds!

•

It's very hard to break through the self-serving blockade of silence and of disinformation, especially in the United States. Miguel is especially attuned to it and emphasizes it; he is very aware of what U.S. public opinion means. He is a born diplomat who lived and did editorial work in the United States for a number of years.

It is very difficult to get out the news (good bad news) of the suffering of these "little people" in our America.

When the "Peace Ship" is captured by ARDE, Edén Pastora's guerrilla organization, on the San Juan River along the Costa Rican border, with U.S. Christians who are also involved in the vigil, an American Dominican here in this Dominican house that has shown me so much hospitality muses, "Miguel D'Escoto fasting for twenty-eight days can't make the news in the States. Twenty-some Americans held for just one day, and immediately it's news there!"

Pastora — Commander Zero, the sad clown who sells himself and sells the whole country for a puff of incense smoke to his self-worship — had threatened to do away with the members of the peace ship should they be sent by Nicaragua on their peace mission. For that reason we deliberately avoided giving them a more formal sendoff, even in the liturgy. They did take part in the Eucharist, of course, like a brigade of evangelizers of difficult peace, and at the end of the mass Miguel and I gave them a small, silent plaster dove.

•

A Brazilian professor who knows a lot about different nationalities and their particular idiosyncrasies said to me (and these days we've talked about it over and over): "The United States — with the wonderful exception of so many thousands of Americans who are fully involved in international solidarity — whether due to their own culpable omission or to inexcusably going along with it, has the best disinformation in the world...." That just proves that being very big and prosperous does not necessarily mean being more human.

That statement may seem harsh and even unjust, depending on how it is taken. The Nicaraguan people, who are so affectionate and generous, are quite capable of making the distinction between the United States government and the American people. "Yankee" means one thing, "gringo" something else, "American" something else again....

•

The patriarch of Nicaraguan literature, José Coronel Urtecho, pays me a visit, accompanied by some poet friends. He did the prologue for a book of my poems, *Cantares de la Entera Libertad* [Songs of Utter Freedom], published by the Central American Historical Institute, the Antonio Valdivieso Center, and the Center for Rural Education and Training. I dedicated the book to Nicaragua as an anthology expressing both urgency and affection:

•

To all the children of Nicaragua
— mother of free men and women and children —
who have shown their willingness to love their Liberty
     unto death.

To all Christian sons and daughters of Nicaragua,
who with the witness of their struggle
and with their hope and their martyrdom
prove that our God is truly a Liberator God.

To all the mothers of Nicaragua,
who have given birth to so many poets, so many liber-
     ators, so many martyrs.

To the free people of Nicaragua,
who whether at work, at a party,
on the border or at prayer,

keep defending their beautiful Freedom, once more under attack from the empire.

To the churches of Nicaragua,
who want to walk like Jesus of Nazareth,
in the simplicity of the gospel of the poor,
and struggle to build God's Reign,
strengthened by the Spirit of the Risen One.

May the Freedom of the New Nicaragua
— of which Sandino dreamed in the mountains —
come to be utter Freedom:
that Freedom with which Christ liberated us.

May the Freedom of the New Nicaragua
leaven the whole liberation
of the New Americas of which we dream.

•

(While I was in Nicaragua this book served me as hands and march-
ing orders and souvenir. In passing it out and writing dedications,
I gave of myself, and something of me stayed behind. The worth
of what is said is measured by how personally charged it is. One
only speaks interpersonally what one says with passion.)

•

Daniel Ortega and some of the other *comandantes* visit me. I
receive them in pajamas and in vigil — and standing up, as in a
state of war.

"If some people saw me in your midst," I kid them, "they would
no doubt be scandalized." (I get my *usted*'s and *tu*'s mixed up.
With my Castilian Spanish I can't get any cordial feeling out of
the aristocratic *usted*.)

"In the midst of such dangerous people as us," adds Daniel
with his cautious and calm manner.

"Anyway, if the pope can meet with Reagan," I add, "I can
meet with you."

•

The war is visible everywhere, even in the smallest details of everyday life. Toilet paper, for example, is in short supply. I had to

write a poem to this scarce toilet paper. A good deal of ingenuity goes into inventing homemade replacement parts. Cars, their tires, and especially busses, offer proof of how precarious things are in Nicaragua under attack.

Mail to other countries is a slow and unsure operation. Central America, they tell me, is engaged in mutual censorship, from one country to another, because the empire has managed to set brothers and sisters against each other.

When he got here Adolfo Pérez Esquivel was horrified at how all Costa Rica has taken a stance of aggressive defense toward Nicaragua. In the plane that brought me here — the "milk run," as they say, because it makes short hops, stopping everywhere — a Costa Rican couple seated next to me put it this way: "Central America's problem is Mexico." I almost fell out of the plane. "Isn't it the United States?" I ventured to ask them.

"Look, the United States has another attitude. The point is that Mexico believes it's better than we are ..."

Praised be the Virgin of Guadalupe!

"Our life here is one of anxiety for peace," a sorrowful peasant told me in the presbytery of León after that first and bloodstained mass I took part in.

A few days later, quite early, almost with the first rays of morning, a young combatant comes to see me, in his green-yellow-brown outfit. He already has a long history, a prophetic one at that, of six years of strivings and journeys. He has heart-rending things to share about faith, about a religious vocation, about militant Latin American struggle. It is an encounter with Grace, and I am deeply moved. I feel the presence of God, who is also an early riser, accomplice in our fleeting hope. The young man has come to bring a wounded comrade to Managua. He has to go back to the mountains right away. I tape some words of peace, a homily in wartime, for the young people in the mountains.

I may never see this young Christian combatant again. And I pray the Lord to go along with him into God's Reign.

●

At strategic points in the city, on the highways, in the mountains, on the border, up and down the country, armed young people — the beloved *compas* [shortening of *compañero*, "comrade," "colleague"], sometimes even *compitas* [diminutive of *compa*], fragile in their violated youth, bring out in me a feeling of impotent paternal tenderness. The constant call for peace makes me feel that the world is quite old and decayed. The youth that prevails throughout this very young population makes me feel old. As though I were on a final mission, at the edge or border of life. On the edge of our church, in any case. The "mountains" and the "border" here are translations of the biblical-existential synonyms of the "desert" and "exile."

•

Cigar in hand, with hearty bootsteps, ever warm in words and ever the dreamer, Tomás Borge pays me a visit. The two of us then go to see Miguel. Tomás talks about the possibility of a "direct invasion" (yes or no). The anxiety of a forget-me-not whose petals people have to pluck every day in this Nicaragua under harassment. He and Miguel have joked about the mouth-watering dreams of a faster. And the *comandante* and priest-foreign minister have also recalled, more seriously, the joke about the prized dog that died while its owner was fasting in seclusion.

This priest-foreign minister is a lover of animals, plants, and paintings. From his ancestors perhaps. In any case, neither the diplomatic war, nor the other war, nor canonical suspension manage to block the human sensitivity found throughout all of Nicaragua with its overflowing affection.

•

By doctors' orders, from both Dr. Juan Ignacio, a *compañero* who is so thoughtful and kind, and the American specialist Kevin Cahill, who was in charge of the team that took care of the pope when he was wounded, D'Escoto breaks his fast. It has been a very intense month with little relaxation. His blood pressure went up several times and from now on he could suffer serious and even irreversible damage.

Those who were accompanying Miguel also break their fast. The Gospel Insurrection is to move into a second phase. These people — here everything is decided in community — also think I will be more useful to the church visiting the communities, speaking with them, consoling them.

It's not that fasting and mission are at cross purposes. Everything has its moment.

In any case, this mini-vigil has touched me deeply. After Nicaragua one has to be different. You can't pass through fire and remain unaffected.

•

Early in the mornings we pray lauds in the Sacred Heart church, which is in the care of the Dominicans. The walls of the vigil room and of the church itself carry the words:

"For peace, against aggression."

"Blessed are those who hunger for Justice."

There are people from communities, some who have come from the mountains or remote areas; priests and sisters; even brothers and sisters from other countries, from these Americas of ours, from the United States, from Europe ...

In the evening in this same church, in the glow of the Gospel Insurrection and of international community in solidarity, we celebrate the Eucharist. Each mass is a challenge and renewal of commitment.

We meet as friends — and I mean really encounter one another; whether we have known each other for a long time or not, we have been traveling together for a long time. These encounters give us encouragement, each one of them like a new living presence of the risen Lord. It is in his name that we meet.

The Gospel Insurrection has become a real event in the Spirituality of Liberation. . . .

On these occasions the "Peasant Mass" (*Misa campesina*) is a must. It says everything, with just the right style. On the day of the Lord's Ascension, when Miguel ends his fast, with pine torches burning and people making public commitments, we launch the second phase of the Gospel Insurrection, going out to the provinces, with an eye toward the International Week for Peace. The composer Carlos Mejía Godoy and his group themselves provide the accompaniment for the "Peasant Mass." In the surging music you find the embodiment of the whole soul of Nicaragua . . . !

That same day is also the premiere of the "Hymn of the Gospel Insurrection," which Miguel D'Escoto and Carlos Mejía have composed together.

The pine torches are lit and we pray the "Litany of the Gospel Insurrection," which I wrote for the occasion and which we will later pray whenever we celebrate in the rural areas. After each invocation the community responds, "Let us light our flame!"

— In the first light of our baptism ...
— In the age-old faith of our people ...
— In communion with the whole church ...
— At home, at work, in study ...
— In the renewed hearts of our young people ...
— In the sacrifice of all those who struggle for Peace ...
— In the spilt blood of our martyrs ...
— In the brotherly and sisterly hope of all Central America, of all Latin America ...
— In the solidarity of millions of brothers and sisters ...
— In the prayer, renunciation, unity, and hope of the Gospel Insurrection ...
— In the heart of the Most Pure Virgin ...
— In the Passover of Jesus ...

Friendly media have been giving good coverage to Miguel's fast and to the more important celebrations of the Gospel Insurrection. *La Prensa*, which complains of a lack of freedom, has been free to insult to its heart's content. About the fast by Miguel D'Escoto, priest and foreign minister, they said sarcastically, "He needed to go on a diet to lose weight"; "It is a desperate propaganda show put on by the Sandinista government"; "It is a way to exit with a flourish and then resign as foreign minister," and so forth. (I'm sorry to discover that that great poet Pablo Antonio Cuadra is part of *La Prensa;* he deserves to be in a more worthy place — for the good of the new Nicaragua.)

A young combatant left this poignant testimony on the desk of Padre Miguel, his foreign minister:

> If there had been more Christians like you
> there would be fewer atheists like me.

•

I have gotten up, in the Managua dawn, already hot, with this conviction bubbling up inside me, like a fountain of freedom: "We have to give the church a good sense of humor."

Nicaragua knows how to laugh, despite everything. The country "doesn't sell out, doesn't surrender," shouts la Chavala* on all sides. These Nicas — so tiny in comparison to the great empire — want peace and dialogue, but "with dignity."

"We're free — now what?" boasts the billboard at an important intersection on the way out of Managua.

Chattering women, market stalls, political slogans, liturgical celebrations of martyrdom and catacomb, and pontifical spectacles in high baroque style are all part of the experience here, one after the other, with a great deal of pluralism — at least on the part of the people.

"Where (the empire's) sin abounded," the grace of solidarity more than abounds.

From now on the Voice of America should be taken as a joke since it lies scandalously. It said the kidnapping of the "Peace Ship"† was a show put on by the Sandinista government. And when Miguel finished his month-long fast, pale and weak, it was the end of "the foreign minister's vacation."

> The Voice of America was saying
> (that's *their* America)
> that the delegitimized priest
> (whom the poor legitimize)
> the foreign minister of Nicaragua
> (that they think is their backyard)
> had now finished his vacation ...
>
> The Voice of America was saying
> that the kidnapping on the San Juan River
> of the Peace Ship, dove poised on the waters,
> of the greatest border in the world,
> was a show put on by the Sandinista government.
> (Look how these Nicaraguans fool around
> even in the middle of a war!)
>
> People should realize
> that this is the Voice of those who have a voice
> because they have their dollars
> and they have the power to kill, with a button,
> the whole human race

---

* "Kid," "young girl"; popular billboard cartoon character who represents the revolution.

† Witness for Peace group kidnapped by contras under Edén Pastora.

and under their own roof the power
to kill, day by day, with counterinformation
their own sickly conscience.

People should also realize
that in the States
August is vacation time.
If you fast in August you're on vacation,
if you go into combat in August you're on vacation,
if you die in August you're on vacation ...

So says the Voice.
Let all the fools on the earth say: Amen, amen, amen.

These days they're celebrating the feast of Santo Domingo (St. Dominic) — "Minguito," the people call him — who is carried down from Las Sierritas neighborhood on a flowered platform to the people praying out in the streets.

I hit on the idea of doing a poem to the three great founder saints all together, who through their sons are all present here in Nicaragua, where the ecclesiastical situation is so turbulent: Francis of Assisi, Dominic Guzmán, and Ignatius Loyola. What would these three have to say about the Nicaraguan ecclesiastical church scene in which their sons — and what great sons all three of them have here! — are involved up to their necks?

•

Toño — Father Antonio Castro, one of the good priests, one who doesn't have a "holy founder" but is also giving his all for people and church in Nicaragua, today — takes me to the Voice of Nicaragua to record next Sunday's gospel commentary. When we come up to the guards at the entrance to the radio station, Toño says simply, like a password, "The Gospel in the Revolution" (the title of the radio program). And like the walls of Jericho, the gates obey and open out evenly before us ...

Another time also with Father Toño I visited the headquarters of the Organization of Disabled Revolutionaries (ORD), which is part of CONARI (National Council for Integral Rehabilitation). The crippled young people took very good care of us, explaining how their organization works and what its aims are. When we went into the shop where the "Third World wheel chairs" are made, the

young man gave this introduction, which I found utterly delightful: "Father Antonio, whom you already know, and *compañero*
Casaldáliga."

One night I come back home, tired, but also happy, and find
on the table a small wicker basket with two flags, blue-and-white
and red-and-black, and some flowers. In a dedicatory note at the
bottom of the basket a mother, Doña Zoila Rosa, asks me always
to remember her two children murdered in the back country: the
daughter, a schoolteacher, the son, a defender.

●

I pay a visit to Coco and David, old acquaintances from the Ecumenical Theological Conference held in 1980 in São Paulo. David's
little girl, four years old, if that, struts in front of the TV set,
shouting, "I'm a cub of Sandino."*

●

A good woman, after a liturgical celebration, compliments me,
without my deserving it: "You have learned Spanish very well,
bishop."

"That's because I learned it as a child, over in Spain ..."

Here I'm completely Brazilian, in all respects; I'm "the Bishop
of Brazil" par excellence. I've never felt more Brazilian.

●

I write letters to Brazil: to my prelature of São Félix, to the CPT
[Pastoral Land Commission] — which is holding its National Assembly, to other organizations. I write to Spain, to my people in
Catalonia. This time writing letters makes me acutely community-
minded. I'm in Nicaragua in the name of many brothers and sisters. Millions of colleagues are here with me. Pedro Tierra,[†] my
buddy, writes to me from the Fifth National CPT Assembly, a
letter-poem, greeting me "with the weapons of Peace," commis-
sioning me to be their "Word," "verse in solidarity," "unleashed
song of brothers and sisters."

---

*Nickname given to troops trained especially to fight the contras guerrilla-
style.

†Pseudonym of Brazilian poet Hamilton Pereira, who was jailed and tortured during the military dictatorship. Coauthor with Casaldáliga of the text
for two masses.

One night I meet with a group that is more or less different: they are called "Christians in the Revolution." Perhaps the name is not very apt since thousands and thousands of Christians are involved in the revolution in Nicaragua. What they mean is that they have an official responsibility in the revolution, a more clearly defined political option, and yet their option for the Christian faith is just as firm. People economically well off, willing to betray their class out of fidelity to the gospel. Teófilo Cabestero has done an outstanding book, *Revolutionaries for the Gospel* (Orbis, 1986), interviewing some of these "different" Christians. Names that are dear for various reasons, distinguished as Nicaraguans and as church people. Names with character and tradition, like the patriarch Emilio Baltodano, the Argüellos, the Vijils, the Chavarrías, the Meneses,... Pinita, Carmen, María del Socorro...

•

Teófilo arrives.* From Panama. In order to write — why else? — the historical and spiritual record of the Gospel Insurrection. Teófilo Cabestero, the pastoral publicity agent, and Maximino Cerezo ("Mino," for short), the painter of Liberation, are becoming providentially indispensable at the most productive moments in the encounter between the church and the revolution. Productive of God's Reign, I mean. (Some time ago the three of us came — to Brazil, Paraguay, Peru — from the old country, Spain, and we have been joined together once more through our publications, often joint efforts, through Latin America, and especially through the Lord in a single ecclesial service of communion. Our missionary streams are drawn into a single channel.)

•

Some Christian communities of Managua have met with the Mexican Jesuit Arnaldo, in order to work out their own way of taking up the Gospel Insurrection.

We talk about the BCCs, the basic Christian communities. Enemies or false friends pejoratively call them the "popular church." (In fact there would be nothing theologically wrong with using that expression if it had not already been branded with mistrust and an apriori condemnation.) BCCs are not some dangerous hankering

---

*Teófilo Cabestrero, Casaldáliga's fellow Claretian.

after novelties; they extend throughout the Latin American church, thank God, and they have more than enough ecclesiastical backing: Pope Paul VI acknowledged them in his encyclical *Evangelii Nuntiandi*. They derive from the first days of the New Testament.

Here in Nicaragua, goes our joint commentary, the very situation of the church and now this atmosphere of Gospel Insurrection force us to reactivate prophecy, which comes out of the very fact of our baptism. In particular we must live out our conversion in daily consistency, always giving upright witness. Let us be sincere, right down to the root. The pine torch has been lit and will have to burn more and more, like a paschal candle in each of our lives.

Christians in Nicaragua — and all Central America — are called on to live more heroically. Overcoming "what is old," being "revolutionaries": in their own hearts, in society, in the church itself. What impels us to be "new men and women" is nothing less than the Spirit of Jesus.

The "collective" dimension that the revolution encourages can quite readily be assumed by Christians in a community manner. Are we not called to create a family spirit?

In the midst of all Nicaragua's battle trenches — military (defense), economic (production), diplomatic and juridical, ideological (consciousness-raising), and the theological trench as well — we will be doing battle with "the weapons of light," being both Nicaraguans and followers of the gospel, faithful to the God of Jesus and to the country of our forebears. Sandino comes in here — why not? — just as our mothers' milk and the blood that has come down to us from those who have gone before. A very old church document, the Letter to Diognetus, described the early Christians harmoniously incorporating Christ into history:

> They are not distinguished from others, either in lands, in speech, or in customs, for they do not live in cities set apart for them, nor do they speak a foreign tongue or live separately from others. . . .
>
> Living and adapting to the practices and customs of each country. . . they take part in everything as citizens, yet they experience everything like foreigners; every foreign land is their homeland, and every homeland is foreign to them.

It is not going to be easy. Christ never said being a Christian would be easy. We will have to carry the cross of renunciation and contradiction. Patiently and freely, combining charism and structure, prophecy and custom, within the church, which is more comfortable adapting and is afraid of what is new. We will have to inject the gospel into the revolution: to be a presence and critical action there, leaven, salt, light. Living "in rebellious fidelity" between community and conflict. Always of course imbibing hope and giving witness to the Resurrection.

We sing. We laugh. And we drink those traditional Nicaraguan cool drinks that so authentically take the place of "their" Coca-Cola.

To the Border

I head off to the provinces, the rural areas, the hill country, the border.

I go to the people, to the communities, to the peasants.
Nicaragua is, above all, the hills and mountains!

> You are quite right
> *compa comandante* Omar:
> "the mountain is more
> than a vast green steppe ..."*

> The mountain is much more!
> The mountain is a whole people
> —ancient green, new green—
> determined to awaken.
> The mountain reaches up to the sky,
> and conquers the city
> and covers over our dead,
> and assures our Peace.

•

Luis Aguirre, father of a family, sharp-eyed, well-built, full heart, is to accompany me on this apostolic pilgrimage. Or I'll be accompanying him (not to be overly clerical). Luis will serve as driver and advisor. He is one of those lay people who have learned to be themselves, freely, within the church of Jesus. As we go along I'm learning about places and what they're called, people and their

---

*Combat memoirs of Sandinista combatant Omar Cabezas (*La Montaña es algo más que una inmensa estepa verde*, Eng. trans. *Fire from the Mountain*. (New York: Crown, 1985). Spanish *montaña* means "hill country," "backwoods," as well as "mountain."

customs, stories and gossip, the communities and their outstanding moments. I kid him and he laughs. And he often laughs at
me. But we've struck up a friendship, one that is both "Nica" and
Christian, and will remain unbreakable.

I've brought a map of Nicaragua with me and I keep it open.
From Pacific to Atlantic, from Honduras to Costa Rica, from Punta
el Rosario to the bay of San Juan del Norte, the Intraturismo logo
opens all of Nicaragua to the traveler as an abundance of beautiful
lakes, mountains, and sun. This time, however, I'm looking for
another Nicaragua ...

•

With flowering malinche trees greeting us on the roadside, Luis
sings to me about the Indian woman, La Malinche, who sold herself
out of passion. These flamboyant red and orange flowers, which
back in Brazil arrive with the Advent rainy season, remind me
more of Christmas. New rows of cotton plants, looking promising,
line both sides of the road we're travelling.

I have just learned, forever, the line from the song

> I'm pure *pinolero**
> Nicaraguan by God's grace ...

We go in to see, with some discretion, the popular hot springs
of San Jacinto, bubbling with cloudy sulfurous water. We came
across them on our way. I'm told I should go see the largest hot
springs at the Masaya volcano. "When peace arrives," as the song
would put it.

While we're filling the jeep at a gas station, three youngsters
come over to me. I'm jotting down my impressions with a ballpoint
and they ask me for it, almost simultaneously.

"It's the only one I have, and I'm going to need it to keep on
writing what I'm seeing here in Nicaragua so that afterwards I can
tell the whole world about it, and so that many friends can help
Nicaragua ... !"

"You're the bishop of Brazil," interjects the little girl. "I saw
you on TV!"

"So, write your name here, on my hand."

And they hold out their little hands, which I solemnly sign, as
though anointing them.

---

* *Pinolero*, from *pinol*, a sweet drink made with corn, means "Nicaraguan."

I'm on the verge of crying. In my heart I vow to get loads of ballpoints and notebooks for the children of Nicaragua who only want to study in peace.

•

A group of young people are meeting at Calasanz high school, which is run by the Piarist Fathers. In the throng is the daughter of Carlos Fonseca Amador,* who has blue eyes like her nearsighted visionary father. From a pastoral standpoint, at this moment, Nicaragua's hour, it is young people who offer the greatest challenge. It is they who have the sharpest expectations that the church will decisively take the right position and will become incarnate in history and genuinely evangelize. They have a right to demand that, and we cannot scandalize them. What is at stake is the future of their Christian faith, which means the Christian future of a whole people, and perhaps of many peoples.

We celebrate mass right there in the patio of Calasanz school, with priests and sisters and people from the communities, and also people from communities near León.

With Father Donald we go to the house of the bishop of the diocese, but the bishop cannot meet with us. He is busy, says the seminarian who receives us, a little flustered.

A U.S. TV crew interviews me. I also give an interview for Hispanics in Brooklyn. Juan Yzuel, a missionary priest from Aragón, will take it with him.

Among other things, I tell Yzuel and his Hispanic community: "... As Christians we have something specific to contribute: faith, the unmerited awareness that there is a greater revolution. We stake our lives on God's Reign, which is more than the Sandinista revolution, since it goes beyond sin, beyond death, beyond our programs and natural aspirations....

"It is this faith that we must 'contribute' to the revolution. And also Christian forgiveness. But that doesn't mean denying this country the right to defend itself. We must be involved in the process in a gospel manner, not like angels.... Christians should take part like everyone else — they too are citizens and Nicaraguans — in production, in defense, in study and cultural activity, in health efforts and popular organization, in criticizing structures, both old

---

*Founder of Sandinistas and main formulator of its ideology, killed in combat in 1976.

and new, since they always need improvement, even within the revolution. Like anything human, the revolution is not perfect....

"We Christians (and especially ecclesiastics) have been trained to 'stand up' to society, standing off from society, although we have in fact thought we had a right to control and define everything as though there were no non-Christians in the world (or as though they were incapable)....

"The church has not gotten along with any revolution, largely because the church as institution, and more specifically, the hierarchy, has almost always gotten along quite well with the established power of the privileged. If we also take the fear of socialism into account, we can understand the ecclesiastical situation in Nicaragua.

"There is a terrible fear that socialism will do away with the faith. (And our theologians tell us that fear is the exact opposite of faith!) There is a tendency to demand that the revolution practically evangelize the people. That's not it's job; that's our job as Christians...."

It is August 14, the eve of the feast of Mary's Assumption. It's the day of the "little roar"; the "big roar" will take place on that most Nicaraguan celebration that takes place on the eve of the Immaculate Conception. During the afternoon the firecrackers ring out repeatedly, warming up the popular festivities. And when the firecrackers run out, because there's no more money to buy them, there are gunshots, gunshots from *compas*, red-hot bursts of shots etching parabolas in the now-darkened sky, and forcing us to come down from the roof of the fathers' house, just in case.

We go out to see the celebration, as well as to sing along, to collect sweets, to savor the people. To blow noisemakers ...

"Why is everyone so happy!"

"The Conception of Mary!"

Conception or Assumption, it's always her, Jesus' mother, who makes us rejoice, because of her Son, the Savior. She also brings joy to the very lively Irishman who is along with us; rolling the "r" is obviously beyond him.

This colonial city of León is full of churches on all sides. "The old cathedral," as Carlos Mejía Godoy's song puts it, "with its carved stone and its swallows, sings to the world the exploits its eyes have witnessed." Oxcarts still occasionally pass through León. With the low houses and cobbled streets, the uproar of this evening makes for a very friendly atmosphere. We stop by here and there as if we were in our own home. Sometimes Father Donald introduces me. I'm "the bishop." I glance around, trying to fit together the different symbols of faith and struggle that each family displays in connection with celebration of the Virgin that they all have in common. The Virgin, Peace, the Revolution, the Pope. Why not all together, each one in its appropriate spot?

In one house, with three women rather advanced in years, apparently charismatics, I suggest that we pray for the peace of Nicaragua . . .

"For spiritual peace, your excellency, for spiritual peace!" one of the women replies, as aggressively as a crusader.

"Of course. For spiritual peace, for family peace, for peace in Nicaragua."

"Look who we've got here!" She shows me the picture of the pope, as though challenging my orthodoxy.

"I also believe in the pope, madam, I do . . ."

We pray. At least it's the same Lord's Prayer. I hope it's the same one, anyway.

●

The sign at the crossroads reads "Mal Paisillo" ["Bad Little Country!"]. Bad for Reagan, this uppity Nicaragua!

"There were five of us mothers of heroes and martyrs, from the time of the insurrection," one woman tells us in Achuapa. "Since January there are now more than forty of us!"

Before mass a little old woman asks me to intercede with the authorities on behalf of two jailed contras. I imagine they're children or relatives of hers. They're not. What's more, over six months ago the contras abducted three of her children and she hasn't seen them since. . . . I have never found such mercy in Israel!

Father Juan is Italian, a missionary of the Consolata order. He's in the right spot to exercise the ministry of consolation. There are several internationalists with him, also Italians (including a very eloquent Italian woman), and a Swiss couple, building a cultural center and a people's hospital. The construction boss from Cremona, a noble soul and a Marxist, admits he has no choice but to believe in this Church of the Poor.

The contras have Achuapa surrounded.

Several relatives of people recently abducted attend the mass.

Some of those present are also wounded. When we join hands for the Our Father, one of them extends his arm all bandaged up. The *compas* stand guard around the church, staked out at the entrance and in the streets. The children come into the sacred precinct, shouting for peace; holding up paper doves, they are like birds themselves. The liturgy of the Assumption speaks of the apocalyptic dragon, defeated by the Woman and her Progeny. Those who have fallen, the wounded, the abducted, their mothers, this whole people, give me the impression that they are clothed in the Christian glory of Mary, who has already triumphed over all the dragons and over death itself.

•

We come to El Sauce, where in fact I intercede with the authorities on behalf of the two prisoners, who have the merciful old woman on their side. One of them will be freed the next day. The other one has already cost Nicaragua many lives and will have to go through the normal trial process, the Sandinista official explains.

I pray that God will always preserve a "heart of flesh" for the revolution. "Generous in (every) victory," generous also "in combat," brothers and sisters!*

We leave Achuapa behind a military convoy. There are five armored vehicles and two trucks. Soon the convoy halts and takes up strategic positions. The machine-guns in the vehicle closest to us go into action. Some peasants, appearing from nowhere, jump out of the woods holding onto long pieces of metal. One feels that the contras are right at hand.... But no — a government truck has run into a pickup on the bridge at the dangerous curve and downgrade near Piedra Grande. We pick up someone injured in the collision and take him to El Sauce.

In El Sauce we make two efforts to visit the priest. He's not in. I leave him a note to express my ecclesial communion with him.

We have a meeting in a people's hall, the kind that the revolution has made available for people who may never have gone into a hall.... *Compas* from a cultural performing group from León sing their own songs, with a lot of feeling, and with guitar accompani-

---

* "Implacable in struggle, generous in victory," was a common slogan when the Sandinista government first took power and had to deal with many former Somoza collaborators. The government did not carry out any summary executions and indeed abolished the death penalty.

ment. The mothers speak, as do some Sandinista young people.

"You mothers," I tell them, "mothers of all these sons who are on 'permanent' defense duty, must also be 'permanent mothers.'"

In Nicaragua, mothers are everywhere, like an overall presence, a primary and ultimate reference point. They go to mass, they go to the hills, they call the people together, they support, they wait. Beloved, tested, strong. Ever the mothers.

> Nicaragua is mothering
> in all directions.

You could begin — and end — a very Nicaraguan poem like that.

"God, mother, peace" are the three words I hear most often in this Nicaragua of mine.

"Revolution" might be the fourth word.

One of these mothers, Doña Silvia Ycaza, one day handed me, as a memorial, some letters, full of suffering and tenderness and strength, that she had written to her son, Roberto Eugenio Sarria Ycaza, "fallen at the age of twenty, in Yalí, Nicaragua, November 3, 1984, a victim of the savage mercenary aggression the country is suffering." One of these letters from this generous mother reads:

Dearest Son,

All of a sudden you went far away, hidden in the mystery of human existence, but you will always be present in my soul, filling this house of yours with joy, brightness, and celebration. I know you are in heaven, still unpacking your backpack, which is full of acts of love and service.

It is very hard, Robbie. Sometimes my suffering tears me apart, but I try to be strong and make hope my life. I remember how affectionate, patient, self-sacrificing, and calm you were, a good student, firm in your decisions, steadfast in your struggle, humble and just like Christ. You made your preferential option for the dispossessed, and in struggle on their behalf you went all the way.

Your committed Christianity would not let you remain a spectator to the injustice and suffering of our exploited peoples, and you were at the forefront of each and every one of the tasks that lead to greater dignity for our people, our blood, our achievements.

You will always live on your soil, in your department at school, in the theater group, in the celebrations you enlivened so much, among your brothers and sisters in blood and struggle, deep within your parents and all of us who knew the way you lived, always dedicated to serving and loving others.

Combatant out of love, hero of your country, adored son, I reverently bow down before you and pay the greatest tribute of admiration and respect.

With a loving kiss,
Your Mamma

The letter is undated, perhaps because it is already eternal.

●

There is a procession in Chinandega, around the churchyard. There will be mass in the Dominican parish church, and a long talk in the hall. The community, from the city and from outlying organized groups, from El Viejo, from the Germán Pomares Sugar Mill, and from Toualá, has a high degree of consciousness and is secure in its faith. The question-and-answer period arrives and I try to respond. I think the Truth makes us free, as Jesus himself said. Lay people, men and women, can and must be adults in the church. These lay people from Chinandega and the surrounding area ask questions about this church that they feel is their own: about different ways of being church, about the pope, the bishops, liberation theology, Leonardo Boff, political commitment by Christians, Christian base-communities....

Eighty percent of all the questions directed at me throughout my two months in Nicaragua will revolve around this church, contradictory and beloved, committed or aloof, a stumbling block or good news.

Sometimes I come to feel that the church is too "present" in Nicaraguan life. As though there were some kind of acute ecclesiasticitis — episcopalitis, someone suggests — preventing a freer and more harmonious presence of the gospel, which would make the church itself present as a free and unsought consequence.

As we're leaving Chinandega, they warn us, "Be careful, Father, this is a dangerous area."

There have been frequent contra attacks in the city and the September 15 radio station in Honduras broadcasts the names and addresses of those who are to be ensnared here. Father Manolo Batalla, who is working very well here in Chinandega, has been personally threatened several times.

•

San Cristóbal volcano is smoking. I look at it again and again with respectful admiration. It is always smoking, this utterly sovereign volcano. I would like to see it at peace with itself... and with its whole neighborhood.

> Don't get excited, San Cristóbal,
> less smoke there, captain;
> though we're headed toward the border,
> we're children of peace.

By contrast, Telica, once a volcano, now rises bare and silent, as though embarrassed over its ancient wrathful outbursts, a stylized outline lost in thought and making one think ...

> Telica, devoid of green life,
> red earth, one big wound,
> pouring down toward the valleys:
> when the dead go silent,
> keep the living awake!
> Don't go silent! Don't go silent!

•

We've scarcely gotten to Somotillo when word reaches us that there are fourteen deaths in Achuapa, the bodies brutally hacked to pieces by the contras. When the contras are surrounded they carry out atrocities, the work of real madmen. They are always inhuman and besides that they are usually on drugs. Around eight people have been abducted in the area of Achuapa. Loose bands of contras in disarray take peasants by force to serve as guides to get them to the border, where they let them go or kill them without pity, like killing a dog that's no longer any good.

The contras must be breaking out toward this area, looking for a way to get to Honduras. We are four kilometers from the Honduran border.

The bridges are guarded by sentry posts.

But the *sacuajoche*, velvety and bright, stubbornly insists on blooming.

Father Angel Arnaiz — who is all commitment and generosity, constantly on the move — and the lay leaders who have taken us in, agree that despite the recent events in Achuapa, we should continue with the program already scheduled. It's wartime and we're going to run into surprises and unforeseen events every day. Besides, they're expecting us in El Ojoche.

We head for El Ojoche, back in the hills, set like a crib scene among steep mountains, a little corner dating back to the Indians, where the clay pots and even the demeanor of the inhabitants still bear the mark of that ancestry. Even the Little Sisters of Jesus — Carmencita, a Salvadoran, and Auxiliadora, whom I know from Brazil — have become potters. As a cherished souvenir of El Ojoche, they give me a chalice and paten, which they've turned with their own hands, bearing the map of Central America. The Lord is alive and challenging in their tiny, and very Latin American, chapel.

In the little houses, set like nests in scrub brush, one still breathes a matriarchal air: in the kitchen the laurel wood grinding board is almost a sacred utensil.

We meet with the Delegates of the Word and the whole community, organized and active, and delightfully rural in their poverty. There is one funny moment. The four militia members chosen to meet and escort us at the opening entrance to the valley go by the bishop's car without seeing him.

"They missed the bishop!"

The delegates are now undergoing a painful testing. They feel they've been undone, as though the very church they have served so generously were officially withdrawing their authority. The dioceses are designating new delegates and catechists, with identity card and everything, strictly official. Perhaps there is going to be an unfortunate ecclesiastical confrontation in the future and — God forbid! — these wonderful lay people will be lost. They are very much a part of the common people, and they have been giving their life for the gospel and for Nicaragua, perhaps for ten or twenty years, since the time when the initiative of peasant Delegates of the Word of God got underway next door in Honduras.

I encourage them to hold onto a free kind of fidelity — for the gospel. Once more we speak about the church, difficult but always ours. These peasants are church, as am I, a bishop. Their great identity card as evangelizers is the baptism they once received. Being baptized means being an evangelizer. Besides, church history is a good guide for being and making church, despite so many regrettable things that have occurred in the ecclesiastical realm.

The mass, in the tiny school, overflowing and hot, the delightful atmosphere of common people, flowers, gestures, the way they drag out the singing, those prayers packed with life, it all brings you to the point of weeping with gratitude. If that weren't enough, right in the middle of the mass a Brazilian priest arrives with Jandir and his associates, carrying a letter from Cardinal Aloísio Lorscheider.*

•

We will not go to Cinco Pinos by the road along the river. That's the danger-filled border itself. But we will still go to the border. These border villages have already repelled contra incursions as many as fifteen times.

When we get to Cinco Pinos late in the afternoon they've just buried two who were killed. There are skirmishes nearby. Some drunks go by in the street, as though they were trying to forget a possibly impending death. The sisters and the *compas* and the people themselves at their doors or on the paths take us in with a friendly and expectant manner. Night falls. At the army headquarters up on the hill, we speak with the remaining combatants; most of them have been outstanding in combat. We talk about peace — always peace! — about God, about the mothers, about international solidarity, about Nicaragua's mission in history. Marta, the young Uruguayan who has a dislocated leg, is a warm witness to this solidarity and of the yearning associated with the cause of Nicaragua in other countries. A very young *compa* puts a beret on my head as a souvenir, a monk's cap, but with other colors: brown, olive green, dull gold.

The army apparently has a force of some five hundred contras surrounded, and a lieutenant has come looking for a loudspeaker in order to encourage them to surrender. For our dinner he brings us a rabbit, still warm; they've skinned it along the way. We help fix the loudspeaker when it finally arrives from Somotillo and I give the lieutenant my flashlight. With all my heart I would like to give him also a greater light, for him, those with him, and all these people who are struggling in the darkness of a malevolent aggression. (Tomorrow, in a trade that is not simply symbolic, the marvellous Sister Pilar will in turn give me a flashlight from Spain

*Head of the Brazilian bishops conference.

with white and red lights, which will delight my backlanders in Mato Grosso.)

We sleep in hammocks in the camp set up by members of a French brigade (including an Algerian) who are building a health center here.

There's a breeze blowing through the camp in the morning. The water faucet and bucket in the patio give me a chance to wash my clothes. The peasant next door draws a young cow over to milk it. The cattle moo, meek and very much a part of the family, while I pray Psalm 35, here so full of meaning:

> Rise up in my defense.
> Brandish the lance, and block the way
> in the face of my pursuers;
> Say to my soul, "I am your salvation.". . .
> For without cause they set their snare for me,
> without cause they dug a pit against my life. . . .
>
> But I will rejoice in the Lord,
> I will be joyful because of his salvation.
> All my being shall say,
> "O Lord, who is like you,
> The rescuer of the afflicted man from those too strong
>   for him,
> of the afflicted and needy from their despoilers?". . .
>
> I . . . put on sackcloth;
> I afflicted myself with fasting. . . .
> As though it were a friend of mine, or a brother, I went
>   about;
> like one bewailing a mother,
> I was bowed down in mourning. . . .
>
> Save me from the roaring beasts; from the lions, my
>   only life.
> I will give you thanks in the vast assembly,
> in the mighty throng I will praise you. . . .
>
> Let those shout for joy and be glad
> who favor my just cause;
> And may they ever say, "the Lord be glorified." . . .
> Then my tongue shall recount your justice, your praise,
>   all the day.

Ministry of Consolation —
Ministry of the Border

On the way out of Managua a large billboard — out of sheer religious concern — proclaims: "There is only one God."

Underneath it someone from the people has added in a very gospel manner: "The God of the poor."

We are skirting Lake Managua, a platter of morning sun, on our way to Granada and the San Juan River.

They tell me the bishops are meeting Tuesday to discuss my being here. I expect that prayer will enable me to get through these events in our church, which take place in the shifting sands of time, in both conflict and mystery.

In the poshest hotel in São Paulo, Pedro Joaquín Chamorro of *La Prensa* has recently given a talk on "Religion in Nicaragua" (that very title), sponsored by Super-Reverend Moon's sect and hosted by João Carlos Meireles, the reigning chief of the business people in the Brazilian Amazon. One day a long time ago the two of us had quite an argument over large landholdings, social justice, and the mission of the church.

The fog presides over this ocean-lake, 180 kilometers long. Next to the port of Granada, the bronze statue of Francisco Hernando de Córdoba, the founder of both Granada and León, donated by the Institute of Spanish Culture, keeps watch or gets bored, in stoic solemnity. Nearby the *compas* in camouflage are talking about incidents of aggression — "They do their harassing from Costa Rica" — while they munch some field rations. Some internationalists from Catalonia say hello, effusively speaking their own language. *"Caram aqui ens venim a trobar!"* "Son-of-a-gun, we meet up way out here!" The vending women shout from the stand where they're selling drinks and fried *empanadas*. I drink a purple-colored drink before leaving. We have a long trip ahead.

42

Since there aren't enough seats on the boat we go on deck. And later we get wet when the waves get rough and rock us noisily. Sometimes passengers on this lake get seasick and even throw up.

Leaning up against Jandir's shoulder, seated on the floor, to kill both time and hunger I pick at the circular rolls Miriam provided. Arnaldo, the Jesuit, has already gone to sleep on a *compa*'s unmoving boot.

When we get to San Carlos at the other extreme of the lake it is night and still raining. San Carlos with the famous garrison, attacked by the young folks of Solentiname.*

Father Lucinio, Sister Reyes, and the *subcomandantes* Alejandro and Bosco, who were once Ernesto's disciples in the Solentiname retreat, are all there to meet us.

We're going to Solentiname. The sky is hooded and we have our hoods up, but we feel the euphoria that goes with approaching a promised land.... †

Solentiname, ah Solentiname!

That night I sleep in Ernesto Cardenal's bed — no small thing! The next morning I preside at the Eucharist, in the company of heroes and heroes' relatives, and wearing the simple cotton shirt that Ernesto has always used for his monastic masses in this green floating monastery. (I will take Ernesto's shirt to Brazil as a magnificent present, and near the heart I will have the word "Solentiname" embroidered in red and black, underlined with green.)

The archipelago exudes a deep peace, but it is on the armed border. The boundary line is out there, green and treacherous. Less than a month ago they discovered a contra plot to abduct Alejandro's wife, Nubia.

I wake up in Mancarrón, the tiny artists' island of the archipelago, beauty on all sides. With the singing of golden orioles — Praise the Lord, golden orioles, praise him all his creatures! — and the national *flor de leche* surrounding the gallery.

There is a permanent encounter with contemplation here on So-

---

*In October 1977, young men from the community headed by Ernesto Cardenal on the island of Solentiname attacked the army garrison at San Carlos in coordination with Sandinista attacks elsewhere. The garrison was destroyed but two of the young people were killed. The Sandinistas regard these attacks as the beginning of the final phase of the anti-Somoza struggle.

†Casaldáliga arrives already familiar with Solentiname, no doubt through the dialogues recorded in *The Gospel in Solentiname* (4 vols., Orbis) and Ernesto Cardenal's poetry.

lentiname, which is now constricted, waiting for daybreak. "When peace comes..." — again the song — Solentiname will once again be the embodiment of contemplation and poetry.

Below, pointing into the lake, is a familiar boat, now old, named "San Juan de la Cruz" [St. John of the Cross].

Don Julio Guevara smiles and plays his unique role as patriarch of the archipelago. José Arana, married to a Costa Rican, is also one of the first, and he describes his experiences to me, low-keyed but accurate.

The chapel is still awaiting the moment when it can be rebuilt. The childlike pictures glow from its ravaged walls. The primitive painters are here in flesh and blood, peasants and fisherfolk. There is a shop producing furniture that is both pleasing and practical. A Peasant Training School to produce quality artists is under construction. But the library is like a huge abandoned wound — Somoza's Guards savagely burned ten thousand volumes!

In his grave Laureano Mairena, the heroic martyr, is guarded by red gladiola bushes, and I have the impression that people greatly cherish his memory. Laureano used to say he was "taking care of my revolution," the way one speaks of taking care of one's mother or children. "And we will continue to take care of it," promises Doña Natalia, mother of Elvis Chavarría, another of the martyrs of Solentiname, along with Felipe Peña and Donald Guevara. "They died in order to live in all," reads the memorial inscription.

Here lay Ernesto. I've slept in his bed.
In this white hammock, of silent lace,
God and the poems swayed back and forth.
I've dreamed the dreams of Ernesto Cardenal and the
  boys.

Out there, on the undivided waters
is the dark green line
   and sister Costa Rica
    (sister no matter what).

The night is raining,
   as though pouring out
    its heart
     — a vessel of memories —
   over our fallen ones
    — chroniclers of hope.

Like a gigantic baptismal font
are you, Solentiname.
Like a gigantic altar.
The heavens on all sides,
on all sides trail and horizon.

From here they set out,
            young eagles of the morning,
to invade San Carlos with freedom.
From here the Gospel,
        set out
            garbed
                as the people.

Garbed alike in love and rustic shirt,
I have drunk His Blood
        with the blood
        of Elvis and Felipe,
        Donald and Laureano.
        ("They died" — with the dawn of day —
        "in order to live in all.")

The little old boat of St. John of the Cross
is going to slip on the sun in order to go its way.
And on the hills the green sprouts of spring
stick up, like a psalm aroused.

While golden orioles
filled my vigiling
hands with song
the island,
the archipelago,
Nicaragua,
Amerindia . . .
I have crossed the night,
the waters of baptism
the dawn of unshakable expectation!
Solentiname,
        sun,
            sun on you, Nicaragua
                Oh, Nicaragua ours!

We head out into the San Juan river on a barge-like boat named

La Puñalada [knife stab], but it's only the wet air and the low clouds presaging rain that raise goose bumps. We may get sprinkled with rain. Paco, our Spanish guide, is both warm and diplomatic, praiseworthy qualities in Spaniards.

The San Juan has been the river most lusted after in Central America, due to its strategic location as an easy route between the two oceans. Conquistadors and pirates, their masts straining, and then landholders and tourists, have gone up and down this San Juan river as they pleased. Mark Twain could plumb many depths of scoundrel behavior and battered humanity in these treasured waters.

The river is about 220 kilometers long, with green all along its banks, and with large farms and ranches here and there among its smooth hills and intermittent valleys. White herons — the same white herons I see in Araguaia — dot the river with stylized dreams of peace.

> Along the River San Juan
> The herons take off, the herons land.
> But by the verdant shores
> like peace — will it come? — they stand.

As if to remind us that peace isn't here yet, a bullet — stray? — whines across the boat from the Costa Rican side. Whether it's from a hunter or a mercenary, no one feels like stopping to check.

This ranch here was one of Somoza's many cattle ranches, then called "Sanpancho," today called "Laureano Mairena." Another, "Santa Fe," is now an agriculture school of the Sandinista Front. Here MIDINRA [Ministry of Agrarian Development and Agrarian Reform] is reorganizing the agricultural life of the country. Peasants have gotten 50 or 60 hectares [123–148 acres] to work individually or, if they prefer, in cooperatives.

This is where they're setting up the African palm project that will take care of Nicaragua's cooking oil requirements. "Unless the mercenaries destroy it for us, . . ." says a worker at the project.

I can understand how the revolution cannot be very pleasing to the landholders since it took away the land they had piled up. Just as it can't be very pleasant for the gringos, since the revolution messed up their fat profiteering from tourism and other means. Over there in Sábalos, the gringos had a hotel.

Spanish greed, English greed, American greed, one after another — always oligarchical greed. It's about time that the rivers of Latin America, the peoples of Latin America, be freed of these greeds of Latin America. For too long the powerful have sucked the blood out of the "open veins" of our Americas!*

•

We get to El Castillo [the castle], El Castillo de la Concepción.

Up above, the old fortress covered with dirty moss is now an army lookout post. Early in the morning, with eyes and hair and the hillside grass still damp, I offer some words of encouragement, freedom, and peace to the young people. Later on we're left speechless in the dungeons, where we find signs of firing squad executions carried out by Somoza's guards.

El Castillo is a the mutilated stump left over from battles, defeats, victories, vigils.

Below is the river with its uneven banks and the strategic wide curve that El Castillo could command. This was the "canal" people had to use, or preferred to use, for getting from one ocean to the other.

Above the river stands the town, its one street wet, set between uneven sidewalks, the comings and goings of housewives and children, parrots and pigs, a pleasant little town. Only a few middle-class types here — charismatics or members of the catechumenate movement, or maybe people just poorly informed — are mistrustful of us. Talking about this group and that and about the United Church and the Assembly of God, one woman explains very ecumenically: "I've never shown disrespect for any domination" (which, less ecumenically, would be "denomination").

The key to the church has mysteriously disappeared. Here Paco's diplomacy comes into play, along with general good will. The key appears and the church fills up, all decked out in baroque style, and we all share in the Eucharist. Very pleasantly, cordially. We take encouragement. We pray and sing, different things, new and old. As we leave mass the seventy-five-year-old self-taught musician shows us the violin he made out of royal cedar and has played for decades.

•

---

*The reference is to the book by Eduardo Galeano, *Open Veins of Latin America: Five Centuries of the Pillage of a Continent* (New York: Monthly Review Press, 1973).

The radio announces that a Jesuit named Jack Donald has been kidnapped in Honduras, apparently in La Ceiba. For his commitment to the poor.

I take a bath using a metal bucket that I lower through some boards into the river. The water sings. And the light of dawn appears.

We have breakfast like priests, like bishops. The people do all they can to serve us. Delicious rice and beans; delicious freshly-made tortillas; white cheese just like my dairyman father used to make; some locally made rolls that taste like communion.

On their walls these holy women have a very ecumenical combination of Santa Lucia and Che, the Last Supper and the FSLN, the Sacred Heart and Sandino, Carlos Fonseca and Julio Iglesias...

"With the Immaculate Conception, we will defeat the aggression," says a poster in Doña Irma's house. This old woman is the widow of a man named Sandino, and her only son is named A. C. Sandino.

The husband of Doña María, who is sick herself, now feels "too old."

Someone driven crazy by war killed one person and wounded three more. The family is still living in great anguish and dire want.

The visits and the contact are a comfort to all of us and make us like brothers and sisters. I've always thought informal visits, with a little faith and human affection, are the most effective kind of pastoral activity.

•

On the way back we visit a resettlement area named "La Esperanza" [Hope] and celebrate the Eucharist. It's a group of people who have been evacuated from a war zone and it looks like everything is on its way, with collective work groups and the cooperative, although it's painful. It's not easy to accept leaving your own bit of land. It's hard to believe that things will be rebuilt.

It's also not easy for the simple faith of these people to exercise discernment in the midst of the contradictions they hear and see and intuit within the church. We try to be discrete and offer only the word and hope. And the body of the Lord.

We go back to the river. *La Puñalada* is obediently waiting for us under the rain as we make our way barefoot through the mud.

•

When we get to San Carlos we're soaked with rain. They lend me some jeans to change into, and a blue shirt that just about fits.

In San Carlos you can no longer carry out ecclesiastical things very officially. The community meeting with the Eucharist will have to take place on the soccer field. Delegations from Los Chiles, La Azucena, and El Laurel begin to assemble there with some people from the town. There are Delegates of the Word and good musicians. Guitars get tuned up and we tune up our spirits, singing the kind of songs that give voice to all the life present in each person and in the whole community. Two lay people give talks. They give wonderful talks, these Christians who are leaders in collectives and in their communities, and who combine their struggle and their faith so wonderfully. The loudspeakers transmit the meeting and some passers-by stop at the entrance to the field. The mass is open, but it has the intensity of a celebration of martyrdom.

As I bid farewell to these people with whom I feel a warm friendship, and watch them head out into an unsure fate, before the arrival of fearful night, I feel a pang in my soul.

> My God, how good the vassal
> Had the Lord been good,

goes a line in the Spanish epic poem *El Cid*. What good Christians these humble folk would be, if we pastors never failed them.

•

The street in the port town, which was burned sometime back, is being rebuilt, and the owner of the bar and restaurant shows satisfaction as she speaks of the work fixing up her establishment. From the balcony there is a marvelous view of the spot where the Frío River and the San Juan River flow together, with boats and barges going back and forth, men shirtless, and birds darting through the air.

In the office of the Sandinista Front there is a pre-Colombian bench, an ancient grinding stone. On Alvaro's wall, once more Laureano Mairena:

> It is our task to fix up the World,
> establish Justice on the Earth,
> carry out the revolution.

We eat family style, with people coming and going, and jokes from Lucinio, a sharp Spanish priest from Palencia. The great painter Pérez de la Rocha, who's also a great talker, ends up with my face on one of those masterful sketches he does so well. Be it known, La Rocha, that's the first time anyone's drawn me from life... you owe me a copy.

> You're kidding yourself, journalist,
> if you think you catch me
> when you snap pictures of me
> as I kiss this coffin.
> I kiss the fallen,
> in the light of history
> under the sun of the pasch.
> I hide neither heart nor flag.
> The dead man is also mine,
> child of my hope.
> His blood is already harvest
> of my unquenchable cry
> > On to God's Reign!

Gilbert has fallen in an ambush near San Miguelito on the property of a reactionary priest. The whole area had already been evacuated as a security measure, at the army's request. Only the priest refused to leave.

Gilbert, a Costa Rican who had become a Nicaraguan citizen, lived twenty flourishing, combative years. His body is waked in El Hogar del Combatiente* without anyone from his family present. The wake lasts all night. The different popular organizations come up to give their homage, all speaking warmly of him. Slogans ring out: "We're free. We'll never be slaves again!"

The loudspeaker plays Nicaraguan and Latin American songs, raising emotions that span the continent: Parra, Viglietti, Chico Buarque...

> Ay, Nicaragua, tiny Nicaragua,
> the prettiest flower of my love
> fertilized with the
> blessed Nicaraguan
> blood of Diriangén... [from *Misa campesina*].

---

*A meeting place and pension for combatants away from home.

We also pray. The gospel of the raising of Lazarus, with the powerful word and deed of Jesus, stamps the definitive seal of hope: "I am the Resurrection and the Life."

Compas, authorities, peasants, women, little girls, the people, all pass by paying homage. I also pay homage. "I am no more than my brothers," neither in life nor in death. I stay behind, still in vigil, in order to pray and pour out my soul with these *compañeros*. Alejandro, Bosco, and Alvaro Reyes take part with emotion: we have to be upright, bear witness, and gather up all this blood being split and put it into building peace and justice, into fruits of new life, within each one of us and for the Nicaraguan people as a whole.

"*Compañeros* are falling every day," ponders Alejandro tensely.

And each death is a human life cut down, and can only be justified by a better life. Into this drama, *compañeros*, brothers and sisters, we must put God, the God of life, with a renewed faith. Only by believing in life can we deal with death.

Neither in Matto Grosso nor in Nicaragua do I get used to these deaths "before their time" . . .

•

There is a long line waiting for the gates to open so people can board the boat to go back across the lake. I get there toward the end. Someone invites me to move ahead but I refuse, of course — a line is a line, for everyone. (Later on, while we're on our way, stretched out in the open on the deck and talking at great length about politics and faith and Nicaragua and Spain and the church, some members of a Basque brigade, men and women, talk about the incident. One of them, who was in the seminary in a religious order and is quite sharp and clever, had been testing me without my knowledge: "You're going to see how even this progressive bishop cuts ahead in the line!")

We set out slowly. A very skilled crew member picks up the buoys in the churning wake.

Perhaps to compensate for the journey over here, the return is delightfully blue. Lake Nicaragua, Cociolba in myth, comes at us in slow waves, like a blessing of peace. We pass by Solentiname, Ometepe, Zapatera, and the volcano peaks Maderas and Concepción. It's always volcanos, or earthquakes and floods and invading empires, one after another. Nicaragua so beautiful and so under attack from nature and from human beings....

The trip is long and allows time to chat with the other passengers, share lunch, nod off in sleep, and meditate.

•

Tola is in the southern part of the diocese of Granada — right in the heart of the committed Nicaraguan church. Tola has stuck in my soul as a commitment I owe out of honor to the gospel. With its green hills, the mountains beyond, the former ranches now become the land of the people, community gardens in the outlying areas which the women who do the work show us, beaming with pride, also the craft work of the women that I take away as a souvenir ... and Gaspar's parish house.

Gaspar García Laviana* shines through Tola and its highways and byways.

We meet in the church with the doors open, the breeze and sun refreshing, while the walls, the altars, the floor and the pews, still smell musty. Delegates of the Word, men and women from nearby communities, the Dominican priests who serve the parish, the Bible we meditate, the Lord who is very present ... and Gaspar. At my side a wizened peasant recalls Gaspar, who taught and sustained him during the decisive moments of the insurrection.

We pray, calmly. The whole church in Tola has the feel of a sanctuary, but one of sheer prayer, of naked commitment.

I once more comment on those two ministries that are so urgently needed in Nicaragua now in order to rescue the church's credibility and the very credibility of Jesus and, ultimately, of the God and Father of Jesus: the ministry of consolation and the ministry of the border.

In order to save that credibility, Father Gaspar gave witness, following out his upright conscience. He loved with that highest love Jesus spoke about, giving our life for those we love.

We go to Gaspar's grave carrying flowers and lighted candles. His delegates, his successors, his heirs. Everyone knows where this guerrilla's grave is.† It is in the town plaza, surrounded by other graves of the heroes and the martyrs, shaded by the branches of

---

*Spanish priest, working in Nicaragua, who joined the Sandinistas in late 1977 and was killed in combat in late 1978.

†Reference to protest song: "The guerrilla's tomb, where, where, where is it?"

the trees, visited by birds and by children. We pray.

I am moved and have little to say. At this moment silence seems to render greater honor. A silence pregnant with greater words.

On the gravestone of the guerrilla priest and martyr are some lines in verse that Gaspar once proclaimed prophetically:

> Off to die, to die
> guerrilla.
> To go up to heaven
> first you must die.

In the parish house we keep talking for a long time. Questions and answers. Challenges. Sharing and communion. Nicaragua, the church, Brazil, the communities, politics and faith. Charging up the batteries of commitment in order to keep moving forward.

Gaspar built this parish house and the community center. This was his library, these his books. Here is his noble Asturian face, the one that challenged the landholders around Tola and inflamed the peasants and combatants, and that saw the Face of God.

Here is his biography, *Gaspar Vive* [Gaspar Lives], written by Manuel Rodríguez García, also a Sacred Heart missionary, who dedicates it to the people of Nicaragua, to his fellow missionaries in Central America, and "to Gaspar, with my repentance, for I was also a doubting Thomas toward him." The Tola communities present me with this biography, in the hands of the mother of someone else who fell, a peasant who was with Gaspar. In the dedication these communities tell me that I have "filled them with hope." I pray the Lord that it be the truth.

Then we have supper in the people's style at La Soya, a restaurant run by Doña Lolita, where Gaspar ate so often. Doña Lolita speaks of him as though he were her beloved parishioner. The restaurant is so simple and pleasant that it could easily be a little pub in Asturias with cider foam spilling on the floor.

We leave Tola, with the feeling that we will have to come back. Gaspar comes along with me. Or calls me. Or accompanies us, now free and triumphant in the Lord.

In my breviary I keep above the text of the Magnificat a shoot with two red flowers, the color of dried blood.

> Like a soaring flight, cut off by death,
> or like a living crucifixion,

like an ultimate embrace, that summons me,
your name is wound about me
Gaspar, brother mine.

Asturian, miner's justice,
rugged cliff
Sacred Heart of Jesus in utter wound.

Tola and its hills will now be silent
— green the war and green the forest —
while we speak together with the God who listens
while the people still keep vigil, waiting
for the Peace of God's Reign, so long in coming.

You and I will speak, Gaspar, by ourselves.
Against the light of my anxious fever.
As though you were already not in glory, already
    arrived.
Heart to heart,
          Gaspar,
                with no other witness
than the Love you now live face to face.

It was landholders
who were strangling your poor people,
who strangle my people.
And it is the same gospel
that caught fire in your hands
more than the ill-fitting rifle,
frustrated love, my brother:
your hands still anointed,
                bleeding,
your eyes crying out to the heavens above.

Tell me, Gaspar,
          what would you do
              if you came back?

And take good care of Tola,
Take care of Nicaragua, still in battle.
Don't let your blood dry up
in the (cracked) chalice of your church.

In Granada, so traditional, the old Granada of the commercial
bourgeoisie, the presentation takes place right in what was once the

main salon of the bourgeoisie. A salon is a salon. The chandeliers and baroque decorations, the layout of the seats and the head table conjure up old-style salons from colonial times. I happen to have diarrhea — but it's under control.

The questions the audience brings up, aimed at me, a bishop of the church, are of searing intensity. I answer with a remorseful heart, since they are a challenge to me as well. What do you say to these mothers "condemned" in their children who fell for their country? What do you say to this girl, torn in two by her desire to remain both faithful to the gospel she learned at home and in school and to the revolution that her family has watered with its blood and that now the church, a particular church, condemns as anti-Christian? How give support to these militant revolutionaries, which the church has abandoned, as though they were off limits?

"Bishop," exclaims one of the mothers, "the priest didn't want to pray over my dead son, because the Sandinista flag was laid over his coffin. My son died for his ideal, bishop. I wasn't going to yank off his flag. I didn't take my son to church but entrusted him to God. . . . I believe in God, I believe in heaven, I believe in hell! Was I wrong, bishop?"

"How could you hand your son over to anyone better, dear sister? To our Father God, who knows how to understand us and always receives us. You entrusted him to the right one."

There are moments when the church pains you like a wound or childbirth.

After the talk, some brigade members from my own Barcelona embrace me and we let ourselves go, speaking in Catalan and figuring out ways to set up solidarity between Catalonia and Nicaragua.

Later on, in one of those funny little tricks life plays, we end up eating in the luxury hotel, whatever it's called . . . Luis grins at me, scoundrel that he is, especially since on the other side of the fancy glass where we're eating, the upper crust of Granada's business sector is also eating, possibly conspiring . . . "So near and yet so far!" . . . I don't know if what Saint Teresa said is relevant here, "When it's time for fasting, fast; when it's time to eat partridge, eat partridge." I do know that Luis applied it to the hilt.

•

On my note paper I keep jotting down loose thoughts, shared confidences, news, verses.

From a mother:

"It's we who continue the sorrow of the Blessed Virgin Mary. She saw her Son sacrificed out of love for the people, to save us from sin."

From another mother:

"I'd like to sit down at the table with Mr. Reagan and tell him, 'Look, we Nicaraguan mothers are suffering a lot in this war. Leave our people in peace....'"

Yet another mother:

"We know it was necessary to hand over our children for the salvation of the people."

A bishop no less, in a clergy meeting, went so far as to express himself in this inquisitorial manner: "Anyone in favor of the revolutionary process is in sin."

La Prensa has this headline on page one: "Popular Church: Atheist and Marxist" (Bishop Bosco Vivas).

I keep thinking that only by giving your life can you say what you believe, what you hope for, the very meaning of your life. My death is my ultimate word.

> ...All at once, with death,
> my life will become truth.

•

In the main plaza of Masatepe, the people have painted a mural: the wounds of one of the fallen bursting into flowers, the mother shrieking, stretching up her hands, and the cross behind, black with sorrow. It's that painting of Mino's so often reprinted and on so many T-shirts all over Latin America. At the bottom, the Nicaraguan soul has placed this beautiful confession.

> Out of this sorrow arises neither hatred nor vengeance
> but rather the will to defend
> the resurrection of Nicaragua.

We celebrate mass in the afternoon on the outskirts of the town under some trees in front of the homemade shrine to the Virgin. A guitar group accompanies the singing during the celebration, and then in the shrine owner's hut, the same group plays the "Corrido de Masatepe" and other folk music. Lots of kids. The same kids found anywhere in Latin America. We have a full supply of young people, with the help of God and with ourselves putting the spark into history!

•

Near Rivas on a side road a community of Guatemalan refugees from Quiché. They left Guatemala in 1982 and they continue to await anxiously the moment when they can return.

When we arrive, they are having a very democratic discussion — with that relaxed and respectful style of genuine Indians — over which of them will go to Panama for a cultural event. Some women are embroidering that wonderfully intricate and colorful Guatemalan cloth.

It starts to rain. We leave the shade trees and go into the rough shed that serves as a community hall. Someone insists, "The women ought to participate also; the women ought to take part in everything."

The mural, composed of old clippings, still red-hot, reaffirms the will to struggle present in this unvanquished people that is both "church of the poor" and "army of the poor."

> We came to struggle
> We struggle for victory.

As I begin the Eucharist I tell them that in my cathedral in São Félix do Araguaia, back in Mato Grosso, which is also an Indian area, I usually celebrate mass with a red embroidered stole that a Guatemalan Indian woman gave me at the Ecumenical Theological Conference in São Paulo. I even composed a little poem to this stole:

> The stole you gave me,
> at each mass, pours
> down my body,
> Guatemala...
> All the Blood of God,
> the blood of a whole people!

The gospel is read by a little girl, in Quiché and Spanish.

I have the impression that the communion is living blood, blood made manifold. "This is the body and blood of Jesus!"

This is the slaughtered flesh and outpoured blood of the people of Guatemala...

The astonishing testimonies we hear confirm it:

"Many children and women are dying there."

"Three of my children were killed," says the little old Indian woman, hunched over alongside her old husband, both of them seeming to gather up in their wrinkled faces many centuries of suffering.

"All my neighbors and friends were killed."

Those "who choose this route" die; "those in poverty" die.

The army abducts and slaughters.

"The Guatemalan government doesn't think that those they're killing are people; they think they're animals.... The only thing that matters to them is the money they're getting. What the U.S. government is doing is unjust. They money they send means more death."

The choral group sings with guitar accompaniment, and the little girl who read the gospel recites for us the "war song," while we all eat — a second communion with deep roots in Guatemala — corn on the cob.

We are deeply moved as we say goodbye. Guatemala is a lot deeper inside us. We give a lift to a young married couple in the community. His spine is broken from a machine-gun wound the Guatemalan army gave him, in full daylight while he was going down a street in the capital of his country.

•

When Reagan, the president of the United States that has such "interests" in Central America, declared a complete economic boycott against Nicaragua, I felt very indignant. And impotent. And I felt the need to shout it out — not so much to him, since I'm quite aware that he wouldn't listen to me, but to whoever could become more aware of this new criminal aggression.

I was on my way from São Félix to Goiânia, and during those thirty some long hours I composed a poem to Reagan, an "ode" taking off from Rubén Darío's ode "To Roosevelt":*

*Rubén Darío (1867–1916), Nicaraguan founder of *modernismo* in Spanish-American poetry, is generally regarded as one of the greatest poets in the Spanish language. In his "Ode to Roosevelt," Darío acknowledges the wealth and power of the United States, but insists that Latin America will resist with its culture and faith.

TO REAGAN

You are being excommunicated by me and the poets,
    the children, the poor of the land:
Pay attention!
We've got to see the world in human terms.
Don't play Nero.
This isn't a movie, you screen monkey:
you're the leader of a great nation!
(I will tell your people to clean off forever
the shit your cowboy boot has tracked over your flag.
And I will tell them, when they vote,
to realize that they may be selling much blood and their
    own honor!)
You may have inebriated the world with Coca-Cola,
but there is still someone lucid enough to tell you "No!"
The profits and power of your weapons
cannot be valued above
the feverish wail
of a little black child.

Empires no longer suit the race of human beings.
Listen, Reagan: the sun
rises as sun for everyone
and the same God rains
over every life God has invited to the celebration.

No people is greatest.
Stay in your own backyard.
Respect us.

Rachel has found you out, Herod,
and you will have to answer for her desolation.

Sandino's star
is waiting for you in the hills
and in the volcano a single heart awakes:
like a sea of indignation little girl Nicaragua
will smash your aggression.

The blood of martyrs holds up our arms
and becomes song and fountain in our mouths.
You have never seen the hills, Reagan,

nor have you heard in their birds the voice of the
     voiceless.
You know nothing of life,
and do not understand the song.

Don't come to us with hypocritical morality,
you mass murderer, you're aborting a whole people and
     its revolution.
The lie you try to pass off to the world (and to the
     pope)
is the worst drug.
You are showing Freedom (in an exclusive screening)
while you block the way to Liberation.

"The United States is powerful and mighty."

All right! "We trust...in God."

You may think you're the owners, you may have
     everything,
even god, your god
— the bloodstained idol of your dollars,
the mechanical Moloch —
but you don't have the God of Jesus Christ,
the Humanity of God!
I swear by the blood of His Son,
killed by another empire,
and I swear by the blood of Latin America
— now ready to give birth to new tomorrows —
that you
          will be the last
             (grotesque)
                emperor!

In Nicaragua someone even doubted that this poem was mine.
It's mine, all right. The Bible has much harsher words for kings
and lords who murdered the poor and sought to take over the
world.

●

From August 26 to 28 there is a seminar, "Toward a Theology of
Liberation from Nicaragua," held under the large thatched roof of
the Centro Valdivieso.

So many friends, so many embraces. Such collective searching, from so many different angles. Following the same compass, we are drawn together in head and heart.

The purpose of the seminar is to discuss a proposal for theological research, which the Centro Valdivieso has decided to carry out during the next few years, with contributions from all those friends and colleagues who are willing to join in the effort. The different pieces of research will be coordinated by Giulio Girardi, who works in the Center.

The seminar is intended as the Center's contribution to the " 'Gospel Insurrection' that has broken out in the country as a result of Father Miguel D'Escoto's fast.... " The aim is to "identify more clearly the *who* and *where* of Christian experience in the revolution, the problems and conflicts posed by this encounter (between revolution and Christianity), as well as the method whereby theology done in Nicaragua can both achieve scholarly rigor and yet be genuinely of the people."

Eventually the presentations and talks of these days and other contributions will be published in several volumes, with Girardi — the ever lucid-pathfinder — doing the editing.

History must be made before it can be written. The church must be made before its history can be written. Mysticism, theology, and pastoral activity must be done first and then reasoned out and refined. One does not live by struggle alone but also by thought. Christians live their faith and think it through, formulating it according to the cultural and scientific resources available in each period and situation.

Someone says that being a member of the Nicaraguan people comes through making a commitment, not through one's passport. They are a prophetic people, I say: by their vocation and of necessity; a people that speaks with its life, that makes others uncomfortable, that rediscovers the demands of faith within the revolutionary process and in relation to a way of being church that it no longer finds satisfactory. Hence the need to exercise the ministry of consolation (the prophets have always done so and the whole church is a "people of prophets") and the ministry of the border (on the geographic border of the country under attack, on the ideological border of politics, of science, of the new critical awareness, and on the sensitive border of the realm of young people). That "the world may believe." That credibility of the church, the name of Jesus, indeed faith in God, may not go under, as a shadowy, useless structure from the past.

•

The slogan is "Get up to date!" [*¡Ponéte al día!*]. Delightful in its Nicaraguan Spanish; demanding and yet utterly normal. One must catch up and be "up to date." Live historically. Put yourself "up to date" with God, who is our daily up-to-dateness. No one can honestly avoid it, and even less a Christian.

> Catch up to date with the Father, friend.
> Catch up to date with the gospel.

> Catch up to date with your heart
> which you must tune to the melody of the present
> just like a guitar for singing
> and anxious all-night vigils.

> Catch up to date with Freedom,
> which is still in flight, my friend:
> a dove that came in from the hills
> and to the hills has returned.
> Catch up to date
> > with Our Day!

•

Apanás is the Germán Pomares Military Hospital, next to the human-made lake on the Tuma River. Functional, green, clean — the hospital and its surroundings. A delightful spot... "when peace comes." (The most lively hospital I've ever seen, although every hospital in the world is, by definition, a bit sad.)

We speak with those in charge and visit the wards, one by one. In every one we encounter a collective smile of relief. Sister Dulcinia promises to bring the wounded boys Bibles. They belong to the BLI [Brigadas de Lucha Irregular, special anti-guerrilla units], who constantly risk their lives. The Nicaraguan "legionnaires." Around their necks they wear crosses and rosaries, and on their young bodies, their wounds and mutilation. In their souls, their anxiety, and their faith as well, and perhaps their bitterness: "I'm a Catholic, Father. It's very painful to find the church against us."

Beside him is his mother. (A good mother doesn't run away, Mother Church.) I sense that both of them are grateful for my presence here as a bishop, like an unexpected sacrament.

Outside, at the inspection post, alongside the usual line of family members paying a visit there is another line in anguish, made up of family members, all inquiring about their combatant, who is perhaps wounded, perhaps dead, still unaccounted for.

The Odor of Death

Stopping in Jinotega on the way back we meet with the Mothers of Heroes and Martyrs organization. We pray together. And we sing. They perform some folk dances of the region for us. A brother and sister, five and three years old, dance with innate grace. The slogan "Inflexible in strategy, quite flexible in tactics" could also mean that during the evil time of war, you have to put on a happy face and turn military marches into dance steps. Despite the attacks, Nicaragua is very joyful: neither selling out, nor surrendering, nor turning sour.

●

We turn toward Ciudad Darío — surrounded by mountains on all sides — to drop off two women who asked for a lift. One of them has a child suffering dehydration. We cross the Darío River and head toward the city of the poet, Rubén.

First come the dogs, the pigs, the turkeys, the domestic animals. Then the little houses and their inhabitants. Your house, Rubén Darío, white and brown. The patio is behind the wall. I come up close to read the white monument to you:

> "I was born in a tiny town or village
> once called Chocollos and now Metapa"
> ...And now Darío!

Rubén's lines, so often declaimed during my literary childhood, swirl about me like a flock of birds. And I give back the patriarch poet his ode "To Roosevelt," now aimed at Reagan. Like an archeologist of emotion, I take a tiny piece of rock out of the wall of his house for my poet friend, Pedro Tierra.

The walls shout slogans. Rubén's own spirit was not restricted to modernism, as some good recent studies under the encouragement of Nicaragua's Ministry of Culture have demonstated.

"Not a single vote for the bourgeoisie!"

"Catch up to date with the victory!"

How I long to eat some corn *rosquillas** in order to savor tradition in this most appropriate place!

Peace! May you see it descend upon your people.

The clouds come down, about to give birth, rolling up around the edges of the mountains.

●

We're on our way to Matagalpa.

Near Los Cardones we pick up Grandma Eufemia. Her granddaughter brought her to the road but she is willing to travel alone.

Doña Eufemia's eye is closing, and her wrinkled skin shows that she's been tossed around for a long time. "How old are you, grandma?"

"Over a hundred."

"Over a hundred?"

"When Tacho [Somoza] came here the last time I was already a hundred... and it's been over ten years since Tacho came!"

Luis, Dulcinia, and I exchange glances as though silently reacting to an interesting film.

"Did you know Tacho, grandma?"

"Of course! I was his cook, on that farm, over there... "

We are in fact passing by La Fundadora, one of the many farms and ranches that the dictator grabbed up.

Doña Eufemia likes the *compas* — she tells us so herself. They have a campsite alongside the road. They all call her "grandma" and give her money so she can buy what she needs.

●

Matagalpa is Carlos Fonseca's city. He was born here in 1936, "out of the very heart of the hardworking populace." A good student, upright, jailed, exiled, martyred. Carlos Fonseca founded the FSLN in 1961, "the very year that Vatican II began," asserts

---

*O-shaped bread made in the region.

the "History of the Church of the Poor in Nicaragua."* Carlos founded the Front "in order to organize the rebelliousness of the people, ever more oppressed by Somoza."

As we go through Matagalpa in the morning, the mist overhead and the river muddy and impassive, we are welcomed by the cemetery set against the hillside.

> Your Matagalpa, Carlos,
> lying under the fog.
> All your people, Carlos,
> still undergoing struggle.
>
> Your river carries blood:
> many bloods made one.
>
> Like an open wound
> the cemetery hears
> the voice of the fallen
> in mute expectancy.
>
> The road is stretching out
> all precipice and curves.
> Your blue nearsighted eyes
> from the heights, watch over
> the hills, combative,
> not a word from La Cartuja.
>
> Santa María bubbles up
> the Pure Fountain bubbles up.
> My heart is weighted down
> with the kisses of the mothers
> and my chalice overflows
> with assaulted grief.
>
> How reply to God, Carlos,
> if I am only questions?

In Matagalpa we celebrate mass in the high school where Carlos took first-place honors. Many mothers of young people who have fallen, led by Doña Esperanza, mother of Ernesto Cabrera Cruz, take part in this Eucharist, which happens to take place on the

---

*Publication in comic book form. The first session of Vatican Council II was held in the fall of 1962.

anniversary of the First Insurrection.* Matagalpa is a town on the
alert. A poor woman present at the mass has given three sons, her
husband, and a nephew to the cause.

In the Eucharist we are celebrating, with Jesus' passover, this
other — gospel — "insurrection." The reading from Deuteronomy
has us choose between life and death, between blessing and curse;
the gospel assures us resurrected life.

Many embraces at the end of the mass; people are very grateful. History is still very fresh, the struggle goes on, and these
people take their commitment very seriously, while they endure
misunderstanding and polarization.

We sleep at the home of Ernesto, known for his heroism and
nicknamed "Cabrerita," an idealist who gave up his life. His por-
trait is all over the house, his name on the lips of all his friends.
Cabrerita struggled wholeheartedly and offers a clear profile of the
"new person." "The main struggle is the struggle against our own
faults. . . . " In the literacy campaign, coffee harvests, the youth organization, the insurrection, Ernesto went all the way: like so many
Nicaraguans and Latin Americans. "Every day more purehearted,
more upright, more grown up, and more a son," his mother Doña
Esperancita would later write of him. These young people are
ready for as high an ideal as can be presented to them. Quite ready
to show that "their ideal is worth more than their life." Ready for
Christ if they see him in a living way and approachable . . . !

I sleep in the same bed where Cabrerita slept, and am happy
to do so — beneath the emblems of his revolutionary passion, his
photos, his diplomas.

In the morning we visit the exhibit organized around the August 1978 insurrection. The sun is out and the paving blocks in
the street are bright, as are the numerous white walls.

> "We have to prepare men who will dedicate not their
> free afternoons, but their whole life to the revolution."

We have to prepare men and women, young people and older people, who will devote their whole life, day in day out, to God's
Reign — which is grace and revolution — until death.

Someone reminds me that Carlos Fonseca's father — the man
who happened to be his father — was an administrator for Somoza,

*Uprising in 1978 in five cities, after the Sandinistas took over the National
Palace in August 1978.

but that his mother was a peasant and maid, daughter and mother of the people.

•

They bring in someone else who has been killed. There have been ambushes nearby. Eight have been killed in Zinica. Seventy contras killed also.

I am surrounded by the odor of death.

Some Sandinista children shout, "We want peace." Anyone with the least bit of human feeling must desire this peace so yearned for in Nicaragua!

The American blockade has affected anything technological in the country. Everything was American here: the electric system, for example. (After all, Nicaragua was a colony.)

But the cypresses of Matagalpa still stand, with Nicaraguan nationality, and they "believe in God"* and keep watch over the dead. So many streets and institutions in Nicaragua and all over Nicaragua bear the names of "heroes and martyrs." The Nicaraguan dead survive in their people, as the poet, Ernesto Castillo Salaverry, foresaw, although he "died without seeing them" (the "schools, cooperatives, hospitals/ bearing the names of those/ who died without seeing them").

•

It gives you an assurance of a certain humble honesty when you hear a *comandante* himself say, "This revolution is a pile of shit!"

Stated like that, with simplicity, with the passion of someone who feels responsible for what happens, recognizes the errors and blunders, and knows that the goal is still a long way off. Stated like an impassioned boyfriend who says "she's so damn jealous," or like a mother, who beams with pride, and says of her son, now getting big, that the "kid is becoming impossible..."

The Kid [*la Chavala,* little girl], as they say here, is just six years old, and things aren't easy. There's no reason to hide that as long as people are willing to go at the challenges of history with tooth and nail and also to face the heavy and monotonous demands of day-by-day life.

---

*Reference to Spanish novel of the 1950s by José María Gironella, *The Cypresses Believe in God.*

Another Sandinista leader showed the same kind of modesty on another occasion when he told me: "The future is unclear and this war is exhausting. Sometimes you can see even people in the Front being worn out."

The revolution isn't finished; it is being built, and it is the people who are building it — otherwise it wouldn't be a true revolution. A people's revolution, that is. The revolution is a work of art, as Fidel Castro likes to say. When it is effective and lasting, revolution means a radical transformation of a whole interconnecting network of political, economic, agrarian, legal, educational, and cultural structures.

There are criticisms, and some are worthy of concern. Just as there are rumors, naturally. And there is social climbing, because some try to take advantage of the general confusion. The *comandantes* aren't all saints, any more than we bishops are all saints.

Carlos Fonseca spoke out strongly against sectarianism, which may be excessive zeal, especially when aggression from outside and complicity within undermine the ideal and the efforts being made for that ideal.

"Sectarianism," said — and says — Carlos, "is the main enemy of unity. We must be careful so we will be able to sift among the different political forces in the country and pick out those who are in line with our aspirations, even to a minimal extent. A sectarian person strives to see only what differentiates and what separates."

Just as we are not born with a Christian heart, we are not born with a revolutionary, Sandinista, socialist heart either. We have to keep revolutionizing ourselves internally, while we are revolutionizing our country, the continent, the world ...

The bishops at Medellín were right on the mark when they said, "there will be no new continent without new people."

•

Peasants, with Indian faces, from the areas near San Ramón are meeting in the school where we are going to celebrate mass. They have fixed up the altar with flowers and decorations in the corridor above the patio. The accordion folds of green hills around valleys compensate very well for the loss of the church space that has been closed to us.

I speak with the person responsible for security, who is leaning against a tree, a discreet distance away. He is a Christian, he tells me, as though for his own relief. Being part of the security forces would seem to be in itself a kind of stigma anywhere in the world.

"Doing a red-and-black" means doing voluntary work. So we are going to do many red-and-blacks of generous service during our life. Voluntarily. Being a Christian is knowing how to serve, in the Spirit of Him whose very reason for coming was to serve and not to be served.

Attending the mass are some *compas* in uniform. Somewhat tired perhaps.

With the mass over the storm breaks out — it held back in very comradely fashion — as the truckloads of people from nearby communities go back experiencing both the rain and their joy. It's risky — both because there's always a chance of a contra ambush and because one of the drivers is drunk and other drunks may also hitch a ride.

There is a lot of drinking in Nicaragua. Perhaps all over Latin America. Some think the tensions resulting from the attacks and insecurity have caused drinking to increase in Nicaragua.

Three of the children in the house where we have supper are in the Front. Near the doorway of the house there is a shelf where various kinds of bullets are displayed like old trophies.

The weather is cool. This area really is cooler.

During the night two foxes cross over the roofs of our rooms.

Tomorrow is the feast day of St. Raymond Nonnatus — from my own land of Catalonia, and the patron saint here.

The old Indian woman, who still has beautiful long hair, waits on us, showing all her experience and attention to detail. She is living here because she was uprooted by the war, by a fire.

•

We go by the health clinic of Susulí. Through Samuladí. Beautiful farm areas, communities slowly taking shape.

In Esquipulas a woman complains about the army, "They took away my three sons, and left me only the youngest..."

"During Somoza's time," adds her cousin, "things were better. You could buy the clothes and shoes you wanted."

I listen respectfully. Whoever had enough money could buy clothes and shoes, I think to myself. I also think how hard it is for a revolution to be accepted by all the people. Revolution demands sacrifice. To consume as you like, when you can, seems to be your right, and that's all there is to it (even though it isn't!). And I think that the prolonged attacks leave people frustrated and disoriented. Is it true that "things were always better in the past..."?

Halfway down the hillsides hovers the mist, fraying at the edges. Cornfields spreading out, and beans among the rocks. Rocky ground is good for beans.

Maryknoll priests, colleagues of Miguel's, are in charge of the parish. The Delegates of the Word are arriving. One of them, Cándido, gives me an assessment of the revolution's achievements. "First, the literacy campaign. Now I read the Bible. I've discovered the Word of God. Before, my life was a mess. Now I play the guitar, singing religious songs. Sometimes some of the *compañeros* even complain because I play mainly religious songs."

The bells ring, the beautiful bells of days gone by, the bells of childhood, the bells of christendom.

In the images in the church there is an enthusiastic display of popular religiosity with its Spanish roots. The Passion of Christ — which in the soul of the people shares popularity with the Virgin — is concentrated on this Black Christ of Esquipulas, which comes from Guatemala, if I'm not mistaken. Above the tabernacle stands a clock — perhaps to mark the hours of the slow agony of the Lord and his poor...

We've slept scattered around different corners of the parish house here in Esquipulas, along with some of the Delegates of the Word, who will leave early. Yesterday we had a mass and supper, all of us together. The workshops didn't take place, but there was no lack of generous harmony and a desire to share, to meet one another. That's a real need for these people who are under attack.

After mass we had a talk. There was no lack of posters and signs for all tastes, with the pope, Obando y Bravo, and Casaldáliga. Previously in San Dionisio a good woman, who sang heartily, after mass led cheers for the cardinal and for me. (What God and the people have joined together, let not the bishops separate....)

We give a lift to some members of a Swiss brigade.

"You were dressed differently," muses a young woman brigade member, more or less at a loss in liturgical matters, who had seen me in full vestments at a celebration in Managua.

A macaw is telling us something, obstreperously talkative here as well. They're called *lapas* in Nicaragua, *araras* in Brazil, and *guacamayos* up and down the continent.

•

We've come to Matiguás by the side road through Muy Muy.

The church loudspeaker is playing music full blast to call the faithful together. We have a talk with the young men training to be Franciscans, and I ask them to be faithful to their forebear, Saint Francis.

We celebrate the Eucharist. We have lunch, enjoying Franciscan hospitality.

"That family seated on that pew over there," a friar tells me, "is one more example of the many families that are divided here in Nicaragua, because of clashing political and religious options." What is true of the Chamorros, to mention a name known worldwide, is also true of other Nicaraguan family names as well.

Is it just the revolution that leads to this kind of division? Or does the gospel itself divide? Or is it the case that there's no way of avoiding either the gospel or the revolution?

•

As it passes through hills that spill down like huge green carpets, bathed in sunlight as they pour into the valleys, the road to Jobo — curves, upgrades, cornfields — is deliriously beautiful. We stop for a moment. To look. To contemplate, in gratitude...

> Eruptions of rocks and greenery
> mountains of Nicaragua,
> accordion folds of shadows and sunlight,
> welcoming delight
> of huts and cornfields:
> on His way through
> He left you garbed in His Beauty.

Still naïve, I let into the jeep a uniformed *compa* loaded down with ammunition and with a bit of booze on his breath as well. Besides that, he didn't really say clearly where he was going.

"That's dangerous," my trip companions remind me. It's not allowed, both because the contras sometimes dress up as *compas*

and because their attacks against vehicles with Nicaraguan soldiers
are especially vicious. For this same reason the peasants in the border areas are generally very tight-lipped, and cordial to everyone,
and they always carry a pang of anxiety in their hearts. Contin-
ual attacks have sparked suspicion in these marvelously beautiful
mountains.

We turn toward La Trinidad — which to me still savors of fallen
young people, premature death.

LITTLE IDEOLOGICAL DIALOGUE

The contras are going against the traffic,
Going against everything, friend!

They're going against the Front
Against life and peace.

They're going against you,
Against the people and against God!*

•

INSFOP [Institute for People's Training] is the documentation and
training center for lay people in Estelí that draws together and
stimulates the life of the communities in the area. They publish
things and organize meetings. It is a resource and a center from
which pastoral concern goes radiating out. It has also cost a good
deal of sweat and blood. It is the product of a long journey by committed people — mainly lay people but also an occasional priest,
such as the marvelous Father Ernesto Bravo — and has suffered its
share of misunderstanding and sometimes even ingratitude.

We sleep in the INSFOP building. A training center can also
be a bedroom, as long as you only sleep there at times when you're
not supposed to be awake...

In Estelí, so often heroic, the martyrs Felipe and Mery Barreda[†]
are all over the place, and there are reminders of them everywhere.

---

* La Contra va a contra mano
¡Contra todo viene, hermano!

Va contra el Frente nomas.
¡Contra la Vida y la Paz!

La Contra irá contra vos.
¡Contra el Pueblo y contra Dios!

[†]Lay couple kidnapped by contras, tortured and murdered in 1982, highly
respected because although they were relatively well off, they devoted themselves to the church, the poor, and the revolution.

With their torches now in glory, they keep alive in these *compañeros* the flame of fidelity. This couple, Felipe and Mery, should be canonized with full voice because of the upright path they followed, surrendering themselves to Christ and the people, to the point of martyrdom.

Saint Felipe and Saint Mery Barreda, pleasant, rendering service, generous even with your blood, pray for Estelí and Nicaragua!

The two Salvadoran nuns in exile are like flustered doves. But they keep fighting "the good fight" that the apostle presented as his greatest claim to fame. Nationality puts no bounds on God's Reign, and persecution stimulates circulation in the blood vessels of committed faith.

Germán, the Mexican priest — wicked like all good Mexicans — makes an important observation: "The exhaustion that no doubt exists in some sectors is compensated for elsewhere by the experience of the revolution in defending against outside aggression. Younger people and those who did not take part in the revolution now have their chance to take a stand for or against it."

Neutral — it would be very hard to remain neutral. In love, in faith, and in revolution neutrality is impossible.

•

It's now September. I write to Brazil again. I ask permission of my church in São Félix to remain a few more days in Nicaragua, for the International Week for Peace and for a retreat a group of friends will be holding right afterwards.

•

Condega has 6,500 inhabitants in the city, and there are six communities in the outlying areas. The patron saint here is St. Raymond Nonnatus, whose mother was dead when he was born ("Nonnatus," "not born") and who went on to be a missionary in the Mercedarian fathers to free slaves.

Four days ago the contras blew up an electrical tower and the town of Condega was left without light or water. A heavy clash just took place nearby. (You could hear the explosions in Estelí.)

Enrique, a Divine Word missionary, serves us a regal breakfast that is more than just in passing, just because we're passing through.

On the door of his room Enrique has put a poster from Mexico with a happy little child surrounded by flowers. The poster reads, "Today is a new day for getting into trouble." A most apt assumption for a priest who is mixed up in these brawls over the gospel and the revolution.

•

Once it was all ocote pine trees from Estelí to the Honduran border, one pine forest after another. Under the protection of Somoza, their ill-born godchild, the Americans hauled everything away, denuding the hillsides and leaving eroded sandpiles. Even the climate of the region has changed. During the first two years the revolution replanted some two million new pines, but the war has interrupted the reforestation program.

Ocotal is suffering drought this year. Since it is high and windswept, it is easily affected by tree cutting. Now people are planting sorghum here; I wasn't familiar with their heads, light brown, as though embroidered. There is also pepper in the yards and entranceways to the houses. *"Chile"* means both spice and joke; a joke is something spicy put into words.

In Ocotal the church and surrounding buildings are huge, like a basilica. Agustín and his fellow Jesuits are in charge. Agustín has a peppery tongue, a great big priestly heart, and a backbone in bad shape.

In the conversation someone recalls Tomás Borge's musing: "Nicaragua is the only place in the world where it's the church that's persecuting the revolution...."

An observation I keep finding confirmed on these wanderings around Nicaragua: everything is seasoned with a bit of humor.

Saint Romero of the Americas, pastor and martyr of El Salvador, is everywhere. And also Che, with his beard and his eyes tested by fire. And, occasionally, Lenin. I've seen Lenin's works in several libraries — donated, apparently more like a decoration or souvenir, perhaps, than something to be read. But always near God, the Virgin Mary, and the holy saints.

In the huge church of Ocotal I have counted fourteen Virgin Marys.

At the turn of the century Nicaragua was still just one diocese and Bishop Pereira y Castellón was "bishop of the diocese of Managua." In any case, all Nicaragua is a little smaller than our

diocese of São Félix do Araguaia, if we're going to measure the
church in meters.

On the poster in the parlor of the huge parish house, beneath
the face of Christ is this beautiful Nicaraguan version of the new
commandment: "Love your neighbor as yourself. Teach reading
and writing."

And on a tree in the plaza, which is lined with stone benches,
there is a plaque recalling Sandino's noble conviction: "Our cause
will triumph because it is cause of justice, because it is the cause
of love."

•

Aranjuez resettlement area. A new settlement. If any settlement
represents a sudden uprooting of a whole group of people from
their own home soil, it is even more uprooted when the settlement
isn't "settled" yet, during these first few weeks when everything is
improvised and everything is piled all over the place.

This handful of families in the Aranjuez settlement is obviously
nervous and displeased. They are all apparently reluctant to speak.
They were brought here by the overwhelming fact of the war, because the contras were active in their area, and because of the unfit
conditions there. But they object — some with words and others
with silence or their looks.

Alfredo, the priest, a foreigner, is one of those people who in-
spires love because they know how to give of themselves. His whole
person shines through his smile. Here he smiles and remains silent;
he knows how to listen; he knows how to wait in a gospel manner.

I also watch myself and first listen a great deal here in Aranjuez.
Then I try to explain things discreetly, respecting what deserves
to be respected. Besides, I'm just passing through.

A settlement leader — Delegate of the Word, heavily under reactionary influence — aggressively complains about the situation.
He criticizes everything: the move, shortages, military service, defense... the revolution. Our friend obviously does not have an
overall vision of politics, of society, of what Nicaragua used to be,
of those who are once more attacking. Besides, two nuns, daughters of a landholder, live and operate in this area, turning the
heads of some simple people. Our friend even says that the church
is asking the government to dialogue with the contras, whom he,
significantly, calls the "guerrillas."

Isidoro was killed this morning. Forty-five years old. He was a militia member. Another *compañero*'s gun went off while he was cleaning it. At Isidoro's wake are his old mother, Doña Rosa — long hair, Indian manner — his two little girls and a group from the neighborhood.

We pray together, with the hope that Isidoro may finally rest in that settlement of utter peace.

•

The town of Murra is a crèche scene. Once it had gold mines in operation. It was also a place with forest reserves.

"It used to be," Petronilo of the radio schools who is along on the trip explains, "that these mountains were a forest of ocote pines. Everything was covered by fog. At eight in the morning it was still dark along this road."

The church is high up on the flat-top mountain, like an eagle's nest. The bells toll out a huge sound, almost violently.

There, near Murra, in these exposed rolling hills, the contras arrived one night while a father, a Delegate of the Word, the mother, and children were praying. The murderers sadistically announced that they had come "in the name of God." And in the the name of this god of theirs and of Reagan, his deputy, they cut off the head of the father and the five children, all under thirteen, right in front of this new mother of the Maccabees. At the mass in Jícaro I would later ask this mother of sorrows to raise the chalice with the Lord's blood while I raised the host of his body.

"Through Him, with Him . . . ; with them . . . with these combined bloods — of the Son and of the children — we give you glory, Oh Father, and we pray for the covenant of your peace!" . . .

The procession through the resettlements ends in Jícaro beneath a torrential rain.

The school children are waiting for us undiscouraged, with placards and branches, and I have to follow them through the streets, with banners, chanted slogans and songs, to the church, which is packed. There we celebrate another Eucharist, one of those that nourish you for many days' journey. At the offertory, all the symbols of land, of work, and of struggle. The mass seems unwilling to end. We are all filling our souls. (The next morning Alfredo says that the celebration made him so happy he couldn't sleep.)

We have supper in the school on school benches, very much in the people's style. And the Sandino Trio, as I name them, plays their whole repertoire, well done, very pleasant. The night even turns romantic.

"You have baptized me with rain from the mountains and skies of Sandino," I tell them.

Sandino set out on his campaigns from Jícaro, and he is very much present in Jícaro. As he is all over Nicaragua, for that matter. The imprint of his unmistakable broad hat is found on flyers and walls. His slight figure is stretched out in giant form, laid out in white stones on hillsides and mountains. "Sandino lives." More than a great historic figure, he is a living mystique.

SANDINISTA BALLAD

August César Sandino
general then and now
don't take off your hat yet
the sun is still beating down.

I've come from your Segovias
and I've felt the attacks,
even children's heads chopped off;
it was the very same attacker,
the very same attacker from the north,
the same then and now!

But also the same,
General, was the courage
of these cubs turned loose
who have been awakened by your call.

Your star was standing guard
in every ocote lookout.
And down from all
the mountains came revolution,
out toward the homeland and the hemisphere;
that was yesterday . . . but now
this time it will be for good.
General, I swear by God!

Doña Simona, who was fourteen then, and worked in the commissaries Sandino set up, gives me a very warm embrace after mass. "Bishop, you look like Sandino."

"I ... like Sandino?"

"He was little too!"

There's more rain that night. Jícaro itself rains, singing and happy in the rain, we seem to be in a musical about countryside and communion.

Bats dart around the boards of the ceiling, their electronic radar turned on, catching mosquitoes, spinning through the silence.

●

In Totogalpa an old lady ponders, "Lots of young people have gone away ... to the mountains."

The girl recalls that today is the anniversary of the death of her brother, who was going out with a group of workers to pick coffee, when the contras ambushed them.

With a Holy Father's wisdom, a woman comments, "Both Miguels [cardinal and foreign minister] are children of God ... and both have a right to pray and fast and invite others to do the same."

●

It's raining when we get to Santa Clara. Alfredo is already waiting for us in the church and other *compañeros,* teachers, students, peasants come filing in. These veterans, who now feel that they have been shoved aside by the hierarchy, show an admirable attitude of faith and service within the church.

Alfredo, a Delegate of the Word, both says this and and doesn't say it. But he goes on, faithful and determined. Guitar in hand. In his short speech he just gave a beautiful definition of the brigade members: "The internationalists are internationalizing love."

●

Mozonte means superb ceramic work, the best in Nicaragua. It is made in the oven, patiently. Up on the hill, as though watching over the road, stands the shrine. The Virgin of Guadalupe must be protecting these areas with their crops and the war, their religious fidelity and ecclesiastical conflicts.

On our way through Mozonte I learn a Nicaraguan saying that helps people endure: "One hour doesn't clear the forest ... "

●

The mass in Ocotal is held in the courtyard of a school named after Leonardo Matute, a young Christian from the area, also a martyr in this cause. Today is the anniversary of his death. Despite the rain, we calmly go ahead with the celebration of the mass. The students and professors are there standing up, as is Leonardo's mother, at my side.

"You're letting the bishop get soaked...!"

The mass has an air of comradely affection and youthful commitment. I look for a way to spur these young people, who are heirs to blood spilt so heroically, encouraging them to be Christians and Nicaraguans in a single authentic whole.

Behind me, presiding over the Eucharist are Leonardo Matute's burning words, so much in tune with Jesus' own words:

> "One who fears death does not deserve to live."
> "What good is life, without freedom?"
> "You find life by dying for others."

That night, in the spacious patio of the parish house we chat for hours with a large group of the most committed Christians. About the church. And the pope. Some of the mothers still feel a wound left in their soul by the pope's visit to Nicaragua which they — and many — see as very unfortunate. We speak about Christian life taken up in simplicity, and become daily fidelity. Questions and answers fly back and forth and touch me deeply. The only way the Nicaraguan people will be able to live their faith — and that means many of the best people — is with critical clearsightedness and no evasion: "yes, yes, no, no," as Jesus required. Getting beyond scandals, separations, misunderstandings, divisions. The result will be a faith purified in a crucible.

"You want me to talk with you about the pope. What I think about the pope, his trip to Nicaragua, how the pope is dealing with liberation theology and Christian communities.

"Well, the fact that the pope is Peter's successor and has the mission of confirming his brothers and sisters in the faith, as Jesus asked Peter himself to do, that is a matter of Catholic faith for all of us. I would give my life to defend this apostolic truth.

"The pope, bishop of Rome, safeguards the unity of the church, spread throughout the world in many local churches, each with its own bishop. Upon this Rock/ Peter, Jesus 'builds' his church, in the sense that he keeps it visibly united in one and the same faith, in the celebration of the same Eucharist, in the communion of charity and in the organization of pastoral services. The true 'cornerstone,' the 'sole foundation' — 'let no one lay down another' — is Jesus Christ himself. The New Testament puts it that categorically, and that is what we Christians all believe.

"The manner and style that the pope has lived and acted throughout history, the way he lives and acts today, that is open to discussion. Peter is one thing and the Vatican something else. The pope could have his curia and his aides — which he needs — in a very different manner. The pope could be pope in a simpler, more evangelical, manner (from our viewpoint, right?), one that would also be more evangelizing.

"You people don't like the Vatican; I don't like it either, as it is. That in no way lessens our faith. We have the right and the duty to want the church to be — and to make it — ever more authentic and a better example. You are also 'the' church.

"Obeying the pope and the bishops doesn't mean keeping your mouth shut in their presence, like little children who have no responsibility, and simply accepting everything they say or do. In the church we should be adults. We are all church: holy and sinful, 'the chaste prostitute,' as some of the ancient saintly fathers of the church put it. If the church makes us, and is our mother, we also make the church, and it is to some extent our daughter — fruit of the Spirit of the Risen One and fruit of our common faith, of our responsible behavior, of our missionary activity, of our service to God's Reign.

"Vatican Council II has providentially rediscovered that the church is the People of God, gathered in Christ. A people journeying toward full liberation.

"This Gospel Insurrection that Nicaragua is now experiencing presses us to move forward more conscious and more committed: we must all 'rise up' in daily personal conversion, in active participation within the revolutionary process itself, and in the ongoing renewal of our church...."

It's the same church windmill, spinning around and around in the distressed minds of these people who are believers, and in my words as a bishop, a wayfarer who still feels quite at home.

•

We head out toward Palacagüina (where Christ was born Nicaraguan).* The car begins to sputter, and the little red warning light is blinking. Father Francisco Lapierre, an advisor to the Christian youth, student, and university movements, rides along with us on one stretch. We talk about the church — what else? He reminds me that not long ago a bishop in Brazil was insisting that the Evil One is present in this world. Isn't the Spirit also present — indeed, much more present? In any case, may the night help us to desire and appreciate the day.

In Managua Father Francisco just met two Christian young men, recently wounded in the hills. Showing him their wounds, they gave a beautiful witness of faith, saying, "It's not for the sake of Sandino, Father. It's for the sake of Christ."

The flu is all around me. It wouldn't be very good for my health to break down while I'm going around like this.

We go into the little village of La Tuna. Today is Thursday. The small community is gathered in adoration before the Blessed Sacrament. In Nicaragua they still maintain the tradition of these adoration Thursdays. "Blessed be the Most Holy Sacrament of the altar." Heat, fervor, and insecurity hang in the air. We chat and pray together; then we once more continue on the road to Palacagüina.

(Ten minutes after we left La Tuna, the contras came into the village.)

In the parish center in Palacagüina, we have another talk with Delegates of the Word and members of nearby communities. About the church, Brazil, the political process, and the demands of our faith. In any case, we must avoid a dichotomy: faith and life should go hand in hand; the Bible and life, as we say in Brazil. If faith goes one way and life another, faith would not be Christian faith nor would our life be Christian. Leaven acts as leaven only if it's inside the dough.

We have a bit of coffee in the local office of the Sandinista Front, and I meet Isabel, a widow three months pregnant. Just a month ago the contras killed her husband, Evaristo Cruz, and a brother in the attack on La Trinidad. Evaristo had already been ambushed three times and had been wounded in the second ambush.

---

*Reference to a song in the *Misa campesina:* "Christ has been born in Palacagüina."

German shows us the site of the grain silos in Palacagüina, which the contras blew up. The contras once burned forty houses here. (That afternoon, shortly after we left, the contras shot down a local man.)

> In evil manner
> at any moment
> around any bend,
> them, the contras.
>
> There stalks death
> beneath their boots.
>
> No debts to anyone,
> everything's paid for.
>
> The hut defenseless
> the mother alone,
> Peace trembles
> like a leaf,
> life is fragile
> with the contras around.
>
> Ambiguously,
> their paths crisscross,
> our *compas*
> and them, the contras.
>
> Night pours
> blood on the dawn
> and the day leaves
> the afternoon red.
> The contras passed by
> killing the day.
>
> Along the borders,
> all of them purchased,
> they, the contras
> go back and forth.
> Those with holy lips
> primly keep them closed.

Land of potters, Condega. Very affectionate people. The mothers, the teachers spare no effort to show their gratitude, showering

me with presents. Clayworking, combative, affectionate, Condega
has molded my heart.

(This business of presents deserves a chapter in itself. And
a boat to carry them. They gave me five belts on these trips —
both Nicaraguan and Salvadoran — to replace the worn out leather
belt which in turn had replaced the belt a group of rowdies from
Rio snatched off me at the end of the Interchurch Meeting of Base
Communities in João Pessoa back in 1978. In the end I gave this old
leather belt to Father Ernesto of Estelí as an apostolic sacramental
in the spiritual retreat we made just before I left. There's no reason
to stick just with the same old sacramentals...)

The church in Condega is solemnly decorated, both the altar
and the pillars. Papal yellow, Nicaraguan blue, and rose red. What
does the red mean? We celebrate the Eucharist with a great deal
of participation.

•

Mist envelops the hills, swallows surrealistically embroider the sky,
and oxen languidly plow away. And on this road of gravel and
rough rocks we have our first flat tire.

Road to Limay, a Stations of the Cross. Crosses for those who
have fallen punctuate the whole distance. Civilians, women, children, victims of mercenary aggression. Nine crosses in one spot
stand in witness to a massacre. Thirty-three people of Limay have
fallen in two months. In the church there is an impressive list of
martyrs. This same night the contras have been in Ceilita, a little
place four kilometers from here.

San Juan de Limay, so neglected before the insurrection, is being reinvigorated in both population and production. This border
road has cost a great deal of economic effort, a good deal of strategy, and many lives. There are many refugees in Limay, especially
Delegates of the Word or community leaders.

"The fact is that they come especially after us," explains Tran-
quilino, who is also a Delegate of the Word. Three of his children
have been abducted and there is no word about them. His wife,
standing beside him, pale with anguish, considers them already
dead.

Some of the refugees crowding into the town are unwilling to go
to the resettlement areas out of fear. The contras have burned resettlement areas several times and have murdered many peasants.

"Enter into the Message" urges a poster tacked up to the church. Enter into the message of Jesus, take the good news seriously.

Sabino and Otilia introduce the eucharistic celebration. The first reading is from the Letter of Paul to the Colossians, chapter one. "It is He who holds the universe together. He is also the head of his body, which is the church. He inaugurates the new life, risen the first from among the dead. . . . God has made peace with the whole world through the blood of his son, poured out on the cross."

The second reading is the Transfiguration of Jesus, from the Gospel according to Luke: "Suddenly there were two men conversing with Him: Moses and Elijah, who appeared in glory and they spoke of his passage, which he was about to complete in Jerusalem. . . . When the voice fell silent, Jesus was there alone."

At the moment of the offertory, in the midst of the other symbolic offerings, an old lady — the widow with the mite — brings a basket of eggs to the altar, just as they are, speckled with chicken dung. Since it is very hard for this grandmother to get down the steps, I ask her to sit on the pontifical throne. "This woman has given more than all the rest." She is seated in the place of honor, in the presbytery.

As we leave the church, the breeze rustles the trees, the roofs, and the imagination, while I listen to the people tell me their dramatic stories:

"It's Mister Reagan who trains them," says one peasant about the contras.

"Their fourteen-year-old son was hauled off in January."

"No doubt there are shortages. I don't blame the revolution but those who are attacking us."

"Most of the people doing defense duty are with the church."

"I always sleep in my military clothes," says a white-haired farmer and old timer.

"I know the gospel reading that says you have to give your life for your brothers and sisters."

These delegates, these sisters, these priests are on the front lines of mission. To neglect, prohibit, or discourage them would mean dealing a severe blow to the advance patrols of the gospel itself.

●

The Way of the Cross in Estelí, led by the Mothers of Heroes and Martyrs wearing white kerchiefs, starts out every Friday from the cathedral plaza. The cathedral itself won't allow them in. Some stations of the cross are marginal, both in the world and in the church.

These stations are for peace. Double file, through the streets. The faith, the singing, the torches waving, and the silence also, undoubtedly rise up to God, and reach deep down into our souls. The stations pointedly link the passion of Jesus to the passion of the people.

At the end, a big bonfire, in front of which Miguel speaks and then I speak. We talk about the stations of the people in the stations of Jesus; of the many sorrowful mothers, of this single road — the road of Calvary — that leads to resurrection, not only of individuals but also of peoples.

A *compa* comes up to Miguel. The contras murdered his mother while the young man was fasting for seven days during Miguel's fast.

Going along with the stations in double file, and pondering so many things jumbled together, feeling some anxiety, challenged by the situation, at a certain point in the road I raise my eyes and read on the T-shirt of the young man ahead of me these lines from Leonel Rugama:

> We've had our chat.
> Now
> it's time to live like saints.

•

Mass in the José Benitez Escobar neighborhood of Estelí with community leaders, committed Christians, pastoral agents, the people. From the mothers to the representative in the assembly. Among them are the son and daughter-in-law of the martyrs, Felipe and Mery. The mass is warm, even physically. The gospel text shows us the disciples at Emmaus. Frustrated by the Master's failure but still able to take in the Pilgrim; disoriented, like the whole apostolic community, but able to recognize the Lord in the gesture of breaking bread.

This afternoon, among his own, Miguel has bared his soul, distressed but strong:

"We have to arouse collective prophecy."

"In everything we do we have to ask ourselves how we're going to explain it to the Lord."

"Thank God for Christ. Thank God we're coming after Him."

"I admit that the church, our church, is to some extent more blameworthy than Reagan. Because it could block it and doesn't."

"...I haven't been able to sleep for three days..."

"The Christian communities are the militant ones in this Gospel Insurrection."

"Call others together and turn up the volume...until we have peace and freedom."

Miguel also speaks about Contadora. Without it the Americans would already have invaded Nicaragua openly. They would have "discovered" the pretext. He talks about the support group, made up of Argentina, Uruguay, Brazil, Peru.

Priest and foreign minister, all in one: "Minister of God, Minister of the people."*

We sing. A Salvadoran refugee plays the guitar, "I who am of the Americas..." In the meeting are some *compañeros* from El Salvador and Guatemala who ask me — and this is the most pressing of all the questions I've faced in Nicaragua — why I don't also go to Guatemala and El Salvador...

I've just gotten — all the way here in Estelí — an urgent invitation from Frei Betto† to go to Cuba. Fidel wants to see me. Why not?

•

Above the Tuma River, an old timer, on lookout. *Compas* here and there, some still children.

THE OLD TIMER

The old timer watches over
the turbulent Tuma's waters.
The mist from the mountaintops

---

*Reference to interviews with D'Escoto and the Cardenal brothers, collected in Teófilo Cabestrero (ed.), *Ministers of God, Ministers of the People: Testimonies of Faith from Nicaragua* (Maryknoll, N.Y.: Orbis Books, 1983).

†Well-known Brazilian Dominican lay brother and writer, whose interviews with Fidel Castro are published in *Fidel and Religion: Castro Talks on Revolution and Religion* (New York: Simon and Schuster, 1987).

like an altarcloth covers
the fallen compañeros.

Alone, he stands watch on the bridge;
the Tuma and his mind without cease
churning, with pain perhaps...
When will there be peace?

LITTLE COMPA

Freckled little *compa*.
How old can he be?
Thirteen at the most.
And, such dignity!
On the bridge he stands
watching the water go by
while the AK and his eyes
stand guard over peace.

The palm trees greet us from the hollow down below and a white layer of fog above the slopes of the mountains calls out for celebration.

At the entrance way to La Dalia a large poster reiterates, "We will continue to be relentless in battle, generous in victory,"

We ask at the regional office of the Sandinista Front if you can keep going. There is combat in this area. In La Estrella we inquire with the special warfare brigade. "Keep the little girl clean," says a poster on the door, referring to one's rifle.

A sign says, "Vietnam."

By the chapel of Guadalupe, where some Christians have come together for the celebration, we have another flat tire. On this road we've had two flats exactly where the contras once ambushed Bishop Salvador Schlaefer of Bluefields on the Atlantic Coast.

Naranjo-Limón. Several adults, two of them community leaders, and six children have been abducted. Others managed to escape.

In 1975 Somoza's gangs murdered more than 150 peasants here. Some were thrown out of a helicopter. Since victory, more than 120 peasants have been murdered by the contras.

Two weeks ago in Zinica, three hundred contras tried to surround thirty *compas* from the local militia. Eight *compas* and more than thirty mercenaries died.

Somoza's Guard had set up a strong presence in Waslala because of the Sandinista guerrillas who were operating nearby.

The Yaosca River, in the area of Zinica, where Carlos died. Now they are planning a large project named "Carlos Fonseca Amador" in this area, to be financed by the European Economic Community....

At night after the community meal, we continue chatting with the leaders about baptism and confirmation, about the bishops and the pope, about our Protestant brothers and sisters. Among other ecclesiastical matters, they want to know just what a cardinal is....

Carlos Fonseca's brother Raúl is in the back of the church. He has the air of a country person about him, and is now a member of the local junta [municipal government]. There is something wrong with one of his eyes; the other eye is blue, like Carlos's.

"It is hard to be revolutionary," confesses Raúl, humbly. (And he speaks about Carlos as though referring to an exemplary master.) "We don't want anyone's death." More than 1,200 contra "soldiers" have been given amnesty this year. "Everyone is sad but the Word of God is living... They won't be able to dump this!" (They won't be able to overturn the revolution that's underway, means Raúl.)

A Delegate of the Word has stated, as though he were discovering something in the faith: "Now we realize that Our Lord Jesus Christ carried out a Gospel Insurrection."

In the meeting the peasants list the different benefits the revolution has brought them: through the agrarian reform and the literacy campaign; through cooperatives and collectives; through schools and health care; through MECATE (Movement of Cultural, Artistic, and Theatrical Expression); through child-feeding programs; through loans for production; through the opportunities and the expression they have now that they never had before.

They are not naïve nor are they fawning admirers. They are quite aware of the limits of the revolution.

Whatever connection this has with the Reign of God comes from them. To what extent is it true that "Between Christianity and the revolution there is no contradiction"?

I can honestly say that I've come away from these Nicaraguan mountains with the conviction that the peasants experience the Sandinista revolution as their own. And they experience the contras — those "champions of freedom" that Reagan canonizes and maintains — as a daily threat, as a mystery of iniquity that has no justification. Occasionally some of them will have trouble telling who are contras and who are *compas,* either because the contras disguise themselves or because of stupidities committed by the *compas,* like all armies. But they know how to make an important distinction: the *compas* kill pigs and chickens, while the contras abduct, rape, and murder peasants, children, and women. More than 300 rural schools have been burned by the contras or have had to close down because they killed the teachers. . . .

Sister Dulcinia took me aside last night to tell me not to say what time we were going to leave or what route we would take. "Here you can't say either when or where you're going, or how you're going to get there." War is war, that's for sure.

In confirmation, as we leave Waslala, two police stop us, "There is a contra ambush on the road. The army is clearing the area. We'll keep you posted." . . .

That the World May Know

It is raining as we return to Managua from the green and treacherous mountains. We come back tired and happy. We are coming back after being with those who are at the heart of the people. Perhaps we helped them believe and offered them a bit of consolation. We are coming back after learning how to hope as only they know how, in their everyday life, under so much strain.

The sun wants to set and is pulling shut the curtain of rain. The cropland, all the beloved Nicaraguan earth, exudes the odor of ripeness, of dignity, of freedom won selflessly.

> Smell of rainy earth
> of self-worth newly won
> Tiny Nicaragua, all ripe
> the justice of your truth
> fills me with freedom
> soil of the heart.

The International Week for Peace is on.

There are *compañeros* from rural areas of Nicaragua and other delegations from fourteen countries of Latin America, North America, and Western Europe, all here in Managua for this week. All over Nicaragua the people follow the Week for Peace through the media and in vigils in their communities. Many other countries in the world, prompted by solidarity committees or by those Christian communities that are more sensitive to the cause of the Third World, have also joined this International Week.

The aim of the week is not to work miracles but simply to cut through the information-blocking process and tell the world the truth about what is happening here; to strengthen or start support committees; to spur celebrations of faith; to arouse concrete solidarity as a result of true communion; to make the flame of the

91

Gospel Insurrection burn forth beyond many borders and despite prejudices and insensitivity.

The Week is for Nicaragua, for Guatemala, for El Salvador, for all Central America. Those of us involved in the preparation and those leading it are emphasizing this Central American character of the International Week for Peace.

•

On September 10 in the Centroamérica School, Sharon, an American from Witness for Peace, and Paolo, member of an Italian aid brigade, give their testimony. The prophet Ezekiel sets the tone. Nicaragua is a time of prophecy while it remains a time of combat.

Sharon weeps, "We have seen these people slaughtered with weapons made in my country!"

Then she gives us her own expressions of hope-filled commitment: "Faith doesn't strive only for the final goal but struggles throughout the whole process.... Life isn't worth living until we find something worth dying for.... Death takes on another context when it's experienced in community.... Now, after seeing Nicaragua, I really want to live — there's a lot to do!"

Paolo has been in Nicaragua for two years, helping as an internationalist. "I only pray to God I won't be indifferent to death and suffering.... We must be witnesses in Europe,... feeling where the roots of contradiction and oppression are.... It can happen that a midwife refuses to kill the children of the oppressed countries (referring to the Israelite midwives under Pharaoh's captivity).... It is the First World that has the biggest debt.... The heroes and martyrs, their names, their presence are building health centers, schooling, life.... The New Person is more collective, more social.... 'May everyone's Homeland be the Earth,' as the Nicaraguan song puts it."

•

Alejandro Bendaña, general secretary of the Nicaraguan foreign ministry, speaks. Miguel, who was due to speak to us, is down with the *quebradora,* a serious flu that seems to have hit Nicaragua with alarming symptoms this year. There's flu going around and also dengue fever, a real epidemic that batters and debilitates your body, leading to hemorrhaging and other complications, and sometimes death.

The World Court in the Hague is dealing with the suit Nicaragua has brought against the Reagan administration. An unprecedented case in the history of that court: a tiny David dares to accuse the giant Goliath.

(The Harvard Law School professor, Abram Chayes, later states that the United States government "conceived, created, and organized" the mercenary forces against Nicaragua. And in the same court the Nicaraguan "ex-priest" and "ex-businessman" Edgard Chamorro, who in fact was director of the Nicaraguan Democratic Force from 1982, also gives a chilling testimony. Revolted by the barbarism and by the manipulation of the CIA — "we even rehearsed the lies we were going to tell," says Chamorro and narrates the atrocities committed — the repentant ex-leader gives his sworn testimony as a historic and eye-opening document.)

Alejandro tells us that the Court's sentence is due in sixty days and that it will oblige the United States to pay damages and compensation. That's the way it would be if justice were really just and applied to everyone.... The United States has already given notice that it is withdrawing from the Court and will not recognize its jurisdiction. Of course it recognized that right when it served its own interests, for instance, when Americans were kidnapped in Iran.

Nicaragua, reply the Yankees, is not seeking justice but propaganda.

Alejandro admits that actually the trial's value will be more political than legal: it will mean moral force for Nicaragua.

"We think," he adds, "that this has to say something to all sensible and honest people in the world. We'd like to think that the twentieth century isn't the eighteenth century." One hundred fifty-six countries signed the Hague Charter. These signatures must have some ethical and social value....

I briefly leave the hall where the activities of the Week are taking place to have a very cordial meeting with a number of brothers and sisters at the Baptist seminary in Managua. Once more, it's clear to me that ecumenism can only become real when its basis is broad faith in the Lord Jesus, this faith pours forth in prayer, and the people are united in solidarity with the poor and with their liberation processes. In the Baptist seminary in Managua at that emotional and family-spirited noontime, the ecumene becomes a reality.

•

I also speak to the participants about "what I have seen and heard," "what I intuit, what I fear, what I hope for."

"I'm taking back Nicaragua's geography in my heart." To indicate that, I do a rundown of the places, the faces, the shared confidences and the events I've experienced during these extremely intense weeks — the same things recorded in these "Notes from an Emergency Diary."

"All of Nicaragua is most beautiful, perhaps even more for me seeing it it during a beautiful season: season of revolution, rainy season." ...

I've had "many meetings with Delegates of the Word, with community leaders; also with Sandinista representatives in many places. Speaking, listening, sharing experiences, and, I believe, sometimes providing consolation. I came away from these encounters committed and consoled."

Such masses are the kind that illuminate and nourish the soul. "Here, as in few other places, I have felt that the Passover of Jesus is the Passover of the People: the death and resurrection of both.

"Nicaragua is happening in the mountains, on the border. That is where the direct attack is occurring and that is where the active resistance, and the peasants' wonderful passive resistance, is taking place. ... What the public sees of the church in Nicaragua takes place in Managua, but the church of Nicaragua is really taking place especially in the mountains and on the border.

"There's a war going on in Nicaragua. People aren't very aware of that in other countries. And maybe even inside Nicaragua people don't always take that into account. Up in the mountains, near the the border, you ask, 'Are you a little more relaxed now?' And they answer, 'Yes, for the last week nobody's been killed and nobody's been kidnapped.' For the last week! In Nicaragua there's a war going on, and it's a war of aggression.

"I said when I got here that I'm convinced that truth is on Nicaragua's side. I've never hidden my political stance. Everyone knows what it is. I've never denied that I have an ideology. In fact, I don't accept anyone saying they don't have one. Of necessity, we all have, and must have, ideology, in order to be complete human beings, 'political animals,' as Aristotle put it a long time ago. I have my ideology, my politics, my passion for Nicaragua and for this Nicaraguan revolution — even though I see its defects, its limitations, and even its sins. Whether they be venial or mortal, God knows and the people will be the judge.

"But even admitting this affection and indeed passion, I can tell you quite calmly, and with a critical spirit, that here you become convinced that the truth is on Nicaragua's side.

"And after travelling through the hills and along the border, and even experiencing the anguish and concern that I feel, I also continue to believe that Nicaragua will be victorious.

"The war is wearing people down, there is a good deal of confusion, but there is a very combative spirit. I have felt that the Nicaraguan people themselves have very much taken on the revolution and made it their own. It's interesting how many Nicaraguans criticize the Sandinista Front and yet love the revolution, with a passion; they criticize the Sandinistas and defend the *comandantes;* they criticize the Front and even the revolution, but at the moment of aggression they take their stand. I have seen many examples of what I'm saying, and you Nicaraguans know it better than I do. I wouldn't be able to say what percentage of Nicaraguans are Sandinistas, but I do have the impression that in overall terms the Nicaraguan people have made the Sandinista revolution their own (and that is an irreversible historic step). 'Thank God and the revolution,' as you people say — and, thank Reagan also, perhaps...

"Amidst these mysteries and these volcanos (I was speaking of the problems and tensions Nicaragua was experiencing) stands the church. The church is a very serious problem today in Nicaragua. Aggression is the number one problem. The number two problem might be the church.... Yes, the church is a problem today in Nicaragua; that is both a source of confusion and a tremendous challenge. Being here has strengthened a conviction I've had for years: this is a crucial locus in the full sense of the word: it is a locus of the cross, it is a theological locus, it is a prophetic locus, and it is a diabolic locus.* Let us hope that prophecy and theology will defeat the devil....

---

*Casaldáliga uses the word *lugar,* a translation of the Latin *locus* (site or place), which is a technical term for the sources of theology, primarily scripture and tradition, but which is understood to include the ancient Christian writers, the liturgy, and the "sense of the faithful." He is thus saying that Nicaragua is a source for theology analogous to the classical sources.

"I could speak about the protagonists of this Nicaragua now in vigil. First protagonist: the Nicaraguan people. I know there is a government, I know there is a Sandinista Front, I know there is a vanguard; but above all else there is a people that is quite conscious and quite united to defend its values and conquests. A people that has its own sovereign self-esteem, and an extraordinary will to achieve independence and self-determination. A people conscious of itself as people that wants to be a people and that will not be prevented from achieving peoplehood.

"I believe that with all the revolution's defects, with all the wearing down and exhaustion, and even with the pluralism that exists in Nicaragua, the Nicaraguan people today are united with regard to the revolution: that means the will to change, to hold onto certain revolutionary achievements, not to allow an invasion, the will to be itself as people. An awareness that they are protagonists of their own history.

"The second great protagonist is the Reagan government. You feel that here in Nicaragua and not just on the Voice of Nicaragua or in *Barricada* or from the mouths of the leaders. No, you sense it in what you hear from the people. The United States government, the president of the United States, Reagan...! (This government, this president, they are attacking us, they are against us, they still think they own Nicaragua!) And the people always make a clear distinction between the United States government and the American people. An American friar was saying a few days ago, that he, a Yankee, felt anger, almost hatred, against his own government, and was astonished that the Nicaraguans didn't feel hatred and were quite clear in distinguishing between the government and the American people.

"The other protagonist (at the service of the second) are the contras. The term 'contras' means many things. Sometimes the word isn't even used. In some places we went, it was in our presence that people first used the word 'contras' publicly. The people speak of 'them,' or in some places more clearly as 'the enemy.' When the people feel more free and more ready for combat, then they say 'the contras' out loud and in public. This reminded me of that religiosity that is traditional in Brazil (in Latin America, among all our old Iberian peoples) that doesn't — or at least didn't — pronounce the name of 'Satan' or the 'Devil.' They spoke of 'the beast' or 'the evil one' or 'the dog.' The same thing happens with the contras. Their diabolical presence is like a mystery of iniquity lying in wait at any moment, around any corner.

"Within the Nicaraguan people, perhaps the most outstanding protagonists are the peasants. Men and women — emphasizing the women, not to please feminists but out of respect for the truth. As is the case throughout Latin America, many Nicaraguan women have become very aware, have taken a stand, have become involved in popular organizations, in the struggle, in the life of the church, to a remarkable extent. And among the peasants, both men and women, there are many unforgettable people who are advancing the Nicaraguan process in their life and work. I single out the veterans of war, those who carried out the guerrilla struggle and today continue as veterans in uniforms that sometimes don't even fit well; peasants who have bravely taken their stand and made their commitment. One of them summed up what they are and what they do, when he told me, 'You see, bishop, I'm a Delegate of the Word, a producer, and a defender.'

"Up there in the mountains they speak more about being 'defenders,' and about 'defense.' They are defenders of the Cause (they defend the church and the revolution with a single life in a connected faith). 'We are defending the revolution,' they say. 'We are defending peace.' Or in a very concrete homespun way, 'We are defending our wives and children.'

"Other great protagonists (most of them peasants) are the Delegates of the Word. The church in Nicaragua should be grateful to God, and some day it may have to say *'Mea culpa'* if it loses the wonderful treasure of these Delegates of the Word. Many of them are men — and that is a treasure since you know that very often it's been the women rather than the men who are in the church. Many Delegates of the Word are remarkable in their sacrifice and dedication, in how they work under such dangerous conditions.

"I should also point out that some religious and sisters, and some priests, are quite heroic. A number of them are foreigners. There's nothing special about being a foreigner, but perhaps there is about being a foreigner and coming to some parts of Latin America. Some Nicaraguan priests are all the more heroic since they are living out their vocation to serve the people at home and can't easily leave. The lives of both are at risk because of the contras, and they may be having a hard time with the hierarchy or with their own congregations. . . .

"I have also been quite impressed with various Sandinista leaders I've met who are in charge of rural areas — specifically a number of women. I have been impressed with their seriousness and dedication and with their exemplary spirit of service to the people. I don't know if Reagan might not have been helpful here also. Reagan has pushed the most conscious, the most revolutionary, the most Sandinista people into a battle trench of greater service and responsibility. These men and women are remarkable — some Christians, others not — real 'evangelizers' of peace and justice, servants of hope.

"The *compas*, the dear *compas:* thinking about them both melts my heart and makes my blood boil. Don't get the idea I'm a warmonger. I don't know how to use a gun, and I'm never going to learn. I think all us bishops and nuns and priests should station ourselves firmly around all the weapons factories in the world and not let a single more weapon be manufactured. Maybe that way we could do away with war, once and for all! But since we Christians believe in eternity, we sometimes let it go for eternity!

"The internationalists. Some might simply regard them as tourists. I don't know what the official view in the United States is. Reagan calls them 'terrorists.' Of course — they terrorize him, and with good reason. The internationalists in culture, in health, in construction, the internationalists in information. . . . Internationalists simply in solidarity. In a chapel in Santa Clara, a Delegate of the Word summed it up: 'The internationalists are internationalizing love.'

"Mothers. Nicaragua is mother. In Nicaragua, mothers, the dear mothers, are in everything." And I recite that poem about Nicaragua, "mothering on all sides."

"Heroes and martyrs. An impressive and moving presence in Nicaragua." I recall what I said in funerals in León and La Trinidad: " 'Nicaragua will survive because as a people it does not forget its martyrs. I'm convinced that a country or a church that forgets them does not deserve to survive.' . . . It is interesting that in Nicaragua people say 'Heroes and Martyrs' together. Who is a hero and who is a martyr? It may be that many are both and in the full meaning of both words. These dramatic testimonies are extremely important and they enrich this long martyrology of Latin America, which can only give rise to peace, freedom, and justice.

"I'm left with many challenges and I want to share them with you, just as I'm left with lots of gifts I've received here, many of them quite moving.

"The revolution faces great challenges. You are aware that, according to official data, 40 percent of the national budget is going directly into defense. Some estimate that, if we also include indirect defense, the percentage may go up to 70 percent or 80 percent. You yourselves can see the roads in Nicaragua, you can see the austerity.... This austerity is a challenge, this weariness that exists and could become more severe; this humiliating situation of centuries of colonization, forty years of fearful Somoza dictatorship. Sometimes it seems that Nicaraguans and especially we foreigners forget that dictatorship. And now these five years of an aggressive war.

"Alongside this powerful and arrogant aggression there is a certain attitude on the part of Holy Mother the Church that is often — and may God forgive me this assessment if it were somehow not true — another kind of aggression, which I cannot really fathom. And this is another great challenge.

"Let me repeat what I've said on various occasions: 'Church of Jesus what do you have to say for yourself in Nicaragua, for Central America and Latin America? What should your gestures, your pastoral stances be here and now?' "

And once again I underscore those two overall lines of pastoral activity here and now: pastoral work of consolation and pastoral work on the borderline. So the church may have credibility and, most important, so the message it preaches may have credibility.

" ...If a great part of the church in old and beloved Europe doesn't want to go to the borderline — because they're tired, because they're contented, because they've forgotten there are other worlds, because they've lost that enthusiasm of the child and of the Christian for creativity and utopia (which in plain Christian talk is God's Reign itself), at least the church is on the borderline here in Latin America, in the Third World, in this Central America, in Nicaragua.

" ...Finally I can see the serious challenge facing international solidarity. Reagan is going to go ahead with his plan, militarily and politically. International solidarity will have to keep coming forth: with prayer, always and above all, denouncing the aggression and the lies of the empire and its stooges and in announcing the truth about Nicaragua, about Central America, and about all of Latin

America. This solidarity will also have to be shown in concrete
and expressive gestures of aid...."

I then tell of my encounters with Sandino and Rubén, with
Carlos,... with Somoza.

"I could also say that I've reencountered myself. As a human,
open to justice and freedom; as a Latin American by adoption and
passionately so; as a bishop of that church that wants to stand
in gospel solidarity with the poor and with their processes; as a
Christian called to give witness to the pasch...."

I finish my talk on this September 10 at the International Week
for Peace, sharing my commitments. Before God and before Nicaragua and before all my brothers and sisters who stand in solidarity with Nicaragua's cause (with the cause of God's Reign here):
"Don't take this as presumption.... I've committed myself to an
extra half-hour of prayer every day and one day of fasting each
week, on Friday. I've made a commitment that in my diocese (or
prelature) each month there will be a day of vigil for Nicaragua
and Central America. And I will ask all those churches or communities that support my coming to Nicaragua to do the same.
I've also made a commitment to come back to stay if there is an
invasion...."

I took on the commitment to write down all these experiences
and discoveries and challenges. And that is what I am doing now
with these pages — on the rush, in bits and pieces — to relate how
Nicaragua is "combat and prophecy."

•

[Casaldáliga here describes his visit to Cuba — where St. Anthony
Mary Claret, the founder of his congregation, was once the archbishop of Santiago. He meets his fellow Brazilians, Frei Betto,
whose interviews with Castro have just been published in Por-
tuguese and Spanish, and Leonardo and Clodovis Boff, both well-
known theologians. He immediately has a three-hour conversation
with Fidel Castro. There are further talks with other Cuban officials, with seminarians, again with Fidel, with the nuncio, with
young people from many Latin American countries discussing the
foreign debt, and visits to museums.]

And in that museum with its memories piled high there also remain
behind, in addition to culture and art, my old dilapidated shoes.

It begins as a joke and ends seriously. They say — Marxists and theologians alike — that these shoes could be the first piece to go into the museum of liberation theology in Cuba.

In compensation, I leave Cuba with my boots on. So be it. And with my boots on I'll have to die.... Along my way, may I ever have God's grace and the people at my side.

•

We return to Nicaragua on the morning of September 14, a national holiday, the anniversary of the battle of San Jacinto against the U.S. invasion. Tomorrow, the 15th, is the anniversary of Central American independence — and that includes Nicaragua.

Miguel, Ernesto, Francisco, and I have lunch together. I mention it in order once more to indicate the apostolic and ecclesial spirit with which these three brother priests, who are blocked canonically, take on their political/pastoral ministry. They are aware that this ministry involves conflict, and also aware that they took it on and continue to exercise it under unusual circumstances. Despite their painful situation they are calm and faithful and, as I see it, they are consistent with the gospel of Jesus and with the priesthood itself. A higher law — the gospel itself — and exceptional circumstances — the situation of Nicaragua — justify an exception to canon law. In fact, such exceptions have been made hundreds of times in the past and also today in the Catholic church with far less justification. These three are also conscious of the new challenge posed to them, on the one hand by the Gospel Insurrection that has been set in motion in Nicaragua, and on the other hand by the powerful reaction on the part of certain high church officials. In addition, Christian communities have new expectations, while the empire and its allies are aiming a new load of political, economic, and military pressures at the Sandinista process, at the church (which these same forces have misrepresented by calling it the "popular" church), and thus against these three, Miguel, Ernesto, and Fernando.

•

I baptize the youngest child of Daniel and Rosario.* They name him after two combatants, close friends and colleagues of Daniel's,

---

*Daniel Ortega and Rosario Murillo, his wife.

who were killed while with him in the mountains. Daniel's mother
and Miguel are godparents. Also attending the paschal celebration
of new life are Jacobo Timerman and his wife. Timerman, an
Argentine Jew, and the well-known author of devastating accounts
of prison and torture,* reminds us with feeling that today is the
Jewish day of Shalom.

●

One afternoon during the Week at the parish of the Sacred Heart
we hold a vigil that is more contemplative, as it were. I read and
comment on the poem I dedicated to Gustavo Gutiérrez, "from the
Amazon of Brazil, in a time of testing and unquenchable hope."
To our "Gustavo Gutiérrez, spiritual master in the highlands of
liberation," for his Latin American guide *We Drink from Our Own
Wells*.

Gustavo's book is eloquent and packed with content, a real
handbook for the spirituality of liberation that Latin America is
living in its best people, primarily in martyrs and the poor, a
spirituality that many of the rest of us also want to live.

Through questions and hints, my poem speaks of this spirituality and its rights. A spirituality that is ours, in continuity with
the Christian spirituality of all ages and all regions. The Latin
American Mount Carmel we can climb and descend — from our
fellow human beings to God and from God to our fellow human
beings — bearing back and forth our sorrows and hopes, our blood
and redemption.

For Nicaragua, within Latin America, the Gospel Insurrection has been — I've already made the point — a providential event
within the spirituality of liberation.

QUESTIONS FOR CLIMBING
AND DESCENDING MOUNT CARMEL

"There's no road along this way."
How long will that be so?
If we don't have his wine
Won't homemade *chicha* do?

---

* *Prisoner Without a Name, Cell Without a Number* (New York: Alfred A. Knopf,
1981).

Will all those who walk with us
last to the light of day?
How can we have fellowship
if we don't even have bread?

What path will you take to heaven
if you don't go along the earth?
For whom are you climbing Mount Carmel
if you go up and don't come back?

Will the oils of the law
soothe old wounds?
Are this King's battles
mere flags or are they lives?

Does the mission take root
in the chancery or in the street?
If you allow the Wind to be silenced
what will you hear in your prayer?

If you don't hear the voice of the Wind
what word will you bear?
What will you give as sacrament
if you don't give yourself in your gift?

If in the face of the empire
you surrender hope and truth
who will proclaim the mystery
of utter freedom?

If the Lord is Bread and Wine
and the Way on which you walk,
and if you make the path by walking,
what path are you waiting for?

There are two major celebrations during the International Week for Peace: a cultural and artistic "Festival of Poetry and Song for Peace and Life" and the final Eucharist.

The unusual festival takes place at the Altamira Theater in Managua. Choirs, peasants, poets, children, from Nicaragua and from elsewhere in Central America: Ernesto Cardenal, Claribel Alegría, José Cuadra Vega, Christian Santos, the National Chorus of Nicaragua, the Guardabarranco Duo, Salvador Bustos, the Gaspar García Laviana Group, the Farabundo Martí Group, the Kin-lalat Group, the Nicaraguan Folk Dance troupe.

No one is being "theatrical" — everyone is expressing life. The Salvadoran child who sings, or the Guatemalan musicians playing, or the mother and poet speaking of her fallen son, send tingles down our spines and into our hearts.

Ernesto recites his poem to "The Empty Shelves" — which are loaded down with the dignity of a whole people. "Sorrowing but joyful over the empty shelves."*

I too read some poems that have recently emerged from the oven of my weeks in Nicaragua.

Never has poetry seemed more beautifully "functional" than tonight; never has singing seemed more "militant."

The final Eucharist also takes place in Sacred Heart parish in the Monseñor Lezcano section. Many priests concelebrate and Leonardo Boff gives the homily:

> Where the poor are, there is the Lord. . . . God is present in Nicaragua in the struggle of the poor. Here is the seed of the new church. . . . The church we form is not abstract but concrete, . . . a new church in a new society, which goes by way of God and also by way of human persons. . . . True followers of Jesus neither surrender nor sell out. . . . We want to take back with us the courage, the bravery of Nicaragua: this people made up of Christians whose history is one of oppression but not of subjection. . . . The church is built on persons, not on rocks. . . . This is a true church because it is a church of martyrdom, an apostolic church. . . .

Leonardo, who is forbidden to do so many things in God's church, is able to preach the homily. In fact he reads from a written text. The warm applause all of us give him is certainly for the the cause of solidarity with the poor, for the committed church, for the new Nicaragua, as he says, sidestepping any honors for himself. But it is also for Leonardo Boff — who is appreciated just as much as he is put off limits — and the same is true of all his generous theologian colleagues, the thinkers of our faith in Latin America.

The mass is truly continent-wide, an expansion in mission to the future, a future of hardship and fidelity. We will lack neither Word nor Blood. Spread over the continent or around the world

---

*Despite the lack of consumer goods, e.g., in the supermarkets, the people are determined to struggle for their dignity.

we will feel united in our hearts, roused to "insurrection" by the gospel.

As *El Nuevo Diario* reports, "at the end of the mass, although it had been announced that Father Miguel D'Escoto would speak, he did not speak, observing the suspension imposed on him by the Vatican. However, he distributed burning ocote branches to each Christian visiting us from the fourteen countries, so that they would keep them burning and spread them around in solidarity with Nicaragua."

•

In Gruta Xavier, a Jesuit retreat house, with a marvelous view of Managua and its lake, professional people, four government ministers, peasants, priests and sisters, homemakers, and one bishop have come together: for reflection and prayer; to find ourselves more tranquilly in the presence of the ever greater God; in order to be nourished by community so as to take on the complex challenges of this period in Nicaragua in a Christian spirit.

It is not always easy to combine contemplation and struggle, and to deal with frustrating reality pleasantly and in a spirit of service. The atmosphere of this retreat is one of searching and conversion, a sincere desire to respond to the Spirit.

Days of prayer and also of tension, over what the future may bring, and over the way the situation is wearing people out. Days of shared confidences. Things like what a militant young peasant with a full beard tells us when we kid him about the love affairs that could be awaiting him during his long periods up in the mountains: "How could I be faithful to God and Nicaragua, if I were unfaithful to my wife?"

During a pause in the retreat, on a trail that goes up to the hill in the Gruta, a father with three sons voluntarily doing defense duty, the youngest of them fifteen years old, asks me, "Do you think we're going to win?"

And one night during that retreat I come across Sebastián (unforgettable Sebastián!), a peasant Delegate of the Word, who at this point has been set apart for a pastoral mission far from his family, with his head against a tree as though to hold in his emotion.

His twenty-four-year-old brother Paulino, married with two children, has just been abducted by the contras in an ambush in

Achuapa, along with other *compañeros,* and all have been murdered. Stunned, Sebastián says the mercenaries pulled out his
eyes and peeled the skin off his face, cut out his tongue, and hung
his body on a tree near the house. "I'm sure that what they were
after was for him to tell where I was; they were looking for me.
And Paulino didn't even know where I was..."

Bearing witness in Nicaragua today provides a daily opportu-
nity for practicing heroism.

Before the Lord and as my personal commitment, I will never
forget all these witnesses I have encountered in Nicaragua.

•

[Casaldáliga decides to accept an invitation to El Salvador for a
one-day visit. "I go empty-handed, somewhat apprehensive, taking
only my pajamas, toothbrush and toothpaste, a ball-point, and a
message." Some days previously, in response to journalists, he
had prepared a response to a recent (August 6, 1985) pastoral
letter of the Salvadoran bishops that seems to legitimize the Duarte
government and to delegitimize the insurgency.]

The letter of the Salvadoran Bishops conference, "Recon-
ciliation and Peace," was necessary; I believe it could have
been prophetic. To my mind it has strong gospel elements....
The letter stresses peace and dialogue, and these are the great
gospel elements that El Salvador is waiting for at this moment and that it desperately needs.

...Nevertheless, it seems that there was no prophetic call
to the party that broke off the dialogue, as there should have
been....It is assumed that there is no sincere intention to
engage in that dialogue. Would it not have been better to
give full encouragement to that intention?

I regret very much that martyr Romero and the many
thousands of martyrs of El Salvador, many of them Delegates
of the Word and community leaders, are absent from the
letter.

I have the impression that even though the letter here
and there speaks in strong terms about violence, it does not
speak clearly enough about the violence of the institutionalized injustice throughout the decades and the centuries in
El Salvador, the violence that is the root of all the other

violences. The very war that El Salvador is undergoing is the fruit of this institutional violence. [The letter] does not speak clearly enough about the crimes of the government, the military, and the paramilitary groups.

. . . [Another very serious error], I believe, is that of recongizing the present Salvadoran government as "institutional," "democratic," and "popular." As we know, this government is the child of a highly anomalous situation and has been set up under conditions that are in no way democratic, under conditions of insecurity and pressure.

The other grave error, one that follows immediately, is, I believe, the unqualified condemnation of a Front, of some [insurgent] forces, supported by many thousands of Salvadorans. By opting for one side, the Salvadoran hierarchy is rendering itself incapable of being a trustworthy mediator between the government and the insurgent forces in El Salvador.

What was written [in the Salvadoran bishops' letter] could have been written here in Nicaragua quite correctly. The Nicaraguan government was voted into office by means of elections that proceeded much more properly than elections in many other countries throughout the world that regard themselves as democratic; more properly, for example, than the elections I have experienced in Brazil for seventeen years. In Nicaragua there is a government elected by the majority of the people and an opposition made up of mercenaries, financed by the Reagan government.

I fear that there is a desire (specifically in Central America) to establish Christian democracy or Christian social democracy as the church's option. I was struck when I saw José Napoleón Duarte's letter in a recent issue of *30 Giorni,* put out by the Communion and Liberation Movement,* which, as we know, enjoys the support of some sectors in the Vatican and of John Paul II himself. In this letter, which looked like the magazine's editorial (on the inside front page), Duarte addressed people in the movement as his comrades. . . .

Since history and God's Reign move on, I hope that this pastoral failure will be repaired through the sensitivity of

---

*Movement explicitly aimed at the "restoration" of elements of the pre-Vatican II church, especially authority.

the church's pastors in El Salvador,... through a renewal of
sincere and open dialogue. And through the will of Christians
to truly stand on the side of the poor in the light of the gospel.
I hope that our brother, Archbishop Rivera y Damas, heir
to the pastoral and martyred legacy of our Saint Romero of
America, will continue to exercise his providential ministry of
mediation. At this moment his mission seems irreplaceable to
me. The power of the Spirit and the protection of Archbishop
Romero will not fail him....

•

Upon arrival in El Salvador my first visit must be to Saint Romero,
to the Divina Providencia hospital, and the altar where he was sacrificed during the sacrifice of Jesus and to his grave in the cathedral.

It amounts to visiting a sanctuary, handling relics. It is a day
of pilgrimage as a bishop and as a Latin American. Like so many
others, like millions, I owe Archbishop Romero the witness of his
life, his sermons, his heroic fidelity to the gospel and to the people, all the way. During the International Ecumenical Theological
Congress, held in São Paulo in 1980, some of us bishops who were
taking part sent Archbishop Romero a telegram, congratulating
him for the very timely letter he had just sent to President Carter.
By the time I received the reply, Romero was a martyr. It was the
last text he wrote while his hands were still mortal. And the last
words he put on this message, as a legacy in the letter, were these
glorious words: "For we believe in the resurrection."

Prompted by his death and that letter, and following a sugges-
tion of Leonardo Boff for the book that Vozes was going to publish
with Archbishop Romero's homilies, I composed this poem, a sad-
ness felt in ecclesial collegiality, a psalm of thanksgiving and renewed commitment, "Saint Romero* of the Americas, Pastor and
Martyr":

> ... You were offering the bread
>   the Living body
>   — the pulverized body of your People

---

*Casaldáliga chooses the startling "Saint Romero" — instead of the normal
Saint Oscar Romero — to take advantage of two meanings of the Spanish word
romero: (1) a pilgrim (one who goes to Rome, from medieval Spanish practice),
and (2) rosemary, both flower and spice (used in cooking and perfumery),
which is regarded as an emblem of fidelity.

> Their victorious spilt blood
> — the peasant blood of your slaughtered people.

... Once again we stand ready for witness
Saint Romero of the Americas, our pastor and martyr!
Romero, pilgrim of peace, almost impossible on this
    embattled earth
Romero, blossoming in the purple of the unvanquished
    hope of the whole continent,
Romero, pilgrim of the Latin American Pasch!

Poor and glorious pastor
murdered by hire
       by dollars
       by foreign exchange
like Jesus, by order of the empire.
... the people have made you a saint...
the poor taught you to read the gospel.

Like a brother
        wounded
           by so much family death,
you knew how to weep, alone, in the Garden.
You knew how to be afraid like a man in combat.
But you knew how to make your word,
               free,
                   ring out like a bell!

And you knew how to drink
the double chalice
         of altar and people
with a single hand anointed to serve.
Saint Romero of the Americas, our pastor and martyr
No one
     will silence
          your final sermon!

Jon Sobrino had also written, asking me to write to Romero to give him encouragement and support. When I got Jon's letter, Saint Romero, in glory, was encouraging us all.

We pay a quick visit to the refugee center at the basilica and then spend plenty of time at the Domus Mariae refugee center. Being with the "refugees" in El Salvador is an unforgettable ex-

perience — crowding, narrow confinement, desperate waiting. The
children hang around my neck and clutch my knees. The people
greet me respectfully when they find out I'm a bishop, but when
they find out I'm also "a friend of Archbishop Romero" they give
me a big hug. The women cry. (Sometimes we all cry a little.)

Relatives of people who have been murdered, disappeared, or
are political prisoners, Christians whose faith is put to an ultimate
test; Salvadorans who seem to have no way out.

"What do you think of El Salvador, bishop? How long is this
going to last?"

"Why don't you also visit the conflict zones, bishop?"

"How come there are bishops and priests who don't live up to
the gospel?"

As a present they give me little wooden crosses painted by
prisoners and sashes and purses that they've weaved. With a dedication that can only commit me more: to stand by El Salvador,
with Central America, to the end.

"Yes I will return," I promise them as one who has an unavoid-
able summons.

Seated in a circle, children sing the ballad of Archbishop Romero, "One March 24th," at the top of their lungs. He is everywhere, Saint Romero, with pictures, one on top of the other, and
on the lips and in the souls of all those children of his ministry and
of his blood.

"At this point it would be offensive to canonize Romero," I
remark to Jon Sobrino. "He's more than canonized!"

We cross Rosario plaza, go through his church, still marked
with the bullets of so many massacres, and come to the gravesite
of Saint Romero of the Americas. The plaques with the names
of those who give thanks, the flowers, and the many thousands of
presences one can feel all around, cover the grave with tenderness
and anxiety. Kneeling in front of it, I ask my holy brother bishop
to make me faithful to the end, free to the end, a pastor to the
end, paschal to the end. . . .

It's five-thirty in the afternoon. We have to finish before seven
since the night is always fearful in El Salvador. In the Archbishop
Romero Pastoral Center, full of students and teachers, sisters and
members of the communities, I speak about God's passing over
Central America. And after many questions and answers — very
much about the matters of most pressing concern to these broth-

ers and sisters — a nun asks me to recite my poem to Archbishop Romero. They all listen standing up, in an atmosphere of emotion, and we all pray the Our Father, and a Hail Mary to Our Lady of Liberation.

"It's been a long time since I've prayed," someone later confesses. "Today I've really prayed."

"Pray for us and tell the pope to pray for us," pleads a young man who has "experienced combat in the mountains."

When asked what message I would give young people I answer, "that you hold on to your ability to dream, that you come closer to the people each day, and that you follow Jesus Christ with a passion."

In the evening Archbishop Rivera y Damas of El Salvador, president of the Central American bishops conference, who has spent the day in San Miguel, receives me quite cordially. He is very sensitive to the challenges of El Salvador and also convinced that the church in Central America has a common task.

Over supper I chat with a community of Jesuit students and I ask them not to fail us, to always stand by the people and to be Jesuits — companions of Jesus. At the Archbishop Romero Pastoral Center I've already asked these people — and also myself — to be poor in order to be free; that they aid us bishops with the truth; that they force us to be closer to the people, in order to be more faithful to the God of Jesus Christ. . . .

Before leaving El Salvador, I write a note to the prisoners.

Dawn appears — it always dawns no matter how dark the night — in that airport so astonishingly "normal." And within my soul, both appreciative and apprehensive, there breaks forth the prayer of old Simeon, "Now, O Lord, you may let your servant go in peace . . . !"

•

I don't know whether I'm leaving. I don't think I'm leaving Nicaragua. I'm staying here. Or Nicaragua is coming back with me. In any case, I'm returning to Brazil more Nicaraguan, more Central American.

It's early morning, September 21. Managua and its warm sun are making me tingle. I say goodbye to the Dominicans in Monseñor Lezcano, who have been so brotherly to me all this time, and I get into a jeep driven by the president of Nicaragua, Daniel

Ortega himself. Reserved and cordial, appreciative and sober, always on duty, Daniel goes out of his way to accompany me. He waits in the airport for two hours and takes me to the ladder of the plane from which I give him and all Nicaragua the trouble-making "V" for victory. Along the way we've been talking about Contadora and international solidarity. In the waiting room Daniel gave me a book of very intense poems by his wife, Rosario, *En las espléndidas ciudades* [In the Magnificent Cities] with these words of dedication:

> "With ever more affection,
> with much, much respect."

There also in the waiting room Daniel has given me more words of dedication on his own book *El acero de guerra o el olivo de paz* [The Steel of War or the Olive Branch of Peace] — basic speeches about the revolution's foreign policy — pulled off a library shelf, the sticker and catalogue number providing evidence of this affectionate theft.

> To Don Pedro
> who has joined his voice to ours.
> Who has linked arms and walked alongside the people.
> United, in the same dreams. With the same hopes.
> Fraternally.

In the waiting room Daniel's children were playing with Joe Power's* children. They played around and ate heartily of the fried eggs we adults passed onto them. The Jesuit César Jerez was also along with us. He and Joe Power had been Miguel's efficient collaborators during the days of fasting and prayer and throughout the Gospel Insurrection, dealing with the media and different kinds of international connections, and planning day-by-day activity.

(As I write these final pages about Nicaragua, "prophets in combat," Joe Power, *compañero* and brother Joe, always friendly and serving others, a fully adopted Latin American, still so young and so willing to live the challenges of this moment in a gospel spirit, has now gone into Peace. He was killed in a bus accident on the highway along with four other people.

---

*An American, a former priest, who married a Nicaraguan and stayed to work in Nicaragua.

Joe, brother Joe: keep helping Miguel, even more efficiently now that you've gotten there. Stay with us, together with so many other *compañeros* who have also arrived. And pass onto our adopted Nicaragua a bit of that supreme Peace in which you now rest forever!)

•

Back in Brazil I write a form letter to give an accounting of my trip to Nicaragua — with a lot of feeling, as names and places pile up in my memory. A single letter, translated and copied, will serve collectively — we've got to learn to collectivize — for my friends in Brazil, Latin America, Spain, the world.

I would like them all to share my experiences and challenges during these days of grace and living on the border. Through prayer and writing, I would like to somehow compensate a little for the impotence that overwhelms me in the face of the arrogance and power of the empire and the heroic weakness of these slaughtered peoples, keeping in mind also the specific individuals — names, faces, and sufferings, the mothers and young people and Delegates of the Word — and the children....

"May any of us who can sit by passively while Central America suffers be cursed by the living God." I write that once more, but now my conviction has become experience and my commitment is lifelong, until death.

Here is how I end my letter:

I don't demand that anyone feel toward Nicaragua the same kind of affection I feel for it, which is even greater now that I have experienced its land, its people, its fiery history. I nevertheless want to express thanks — in the name of that same Nicaragua that repeatedly asked me to do so — for the support you gave me in this journey of communion. In addition, I ask of you, brothers and sisters and *compañeros*, that you show real solidarity with Nicaragua and with all Central America. I ask those bishop colleagues who gave me public support to invite their churches to a monthly day of vigil for Nicaragua and for Central America. I ask everyone to join solidarity committees and to cooperate effectively in the campaigns that are organized.... I ask everyone to stay informed and to inform others. We have to break through the blockade of silence and lies. Let our denunciation be heard. Let the news be heard: the bad-good-news of death and resurrection our Central American brothers and sisters are undergoing. Their blood — poor and generous — must fall into our hearts, becoming Eucharist.

Let us make our own the prophetic statement of a Nicaraguan, a survivor of Wiwilí, who, transfixed with grief, told Teófilo Cabestrero, "I survived to tell about it, so that the story will be told and the world may know."